Understanding Sensory Processing Challenges

A Workbook for Children and Teens

Robert Jason Grant

AutPlay® Publishing

Understanding Sensory Processing Challenges
A Workbook for Children and Teens

©2018 Robert Jason Grant Ed.D
Springfield, Missouri: AutPlay® Publishing
A Robert Jason Grant Ed.D Product

ISBN: 978-0-9882718-9-0

All Images Provided by ClipArtLord.com and Robert Jason Grant Ed.D

Correspondence regarding this book:
Robert Jason Grant Ed.D/AutPlay Publishing
DrGrant@robertjasongrant.com
info@autplaytherapy.com
www.robertjasongrant.com
www.autplaytherapy.com

In Memory of

Dr. Mistie Dawn Barnes

June 25, 1976 - August 4, 2017

"Seashells remind us that every passing life leaves something beautiful behind." Unknown

*"Keep your face always toward the sunshine –
and shadows will fall behind you."*
— Walt Whitman

What Others Are Saying

As a play therapist who works with many children daily, sensory processing disorder is becoming more prevalent in the world. Robert Jason Grant's book, Understanding Sensory Processing Challenges: A Workbook for Children and Teens is a must have! This workbook could be worked through session-by-session, individually, or in a group setting. The activities can be used in a stand-alone format, depending on the specific situation of the child. Dr. Grant provides an excellent, easy to read, and thorough explanation of sensory processing disorder and treatment options. The fun and playful techniques, offered by several top-notch clinicians in the country, can be incorporated easily to help in treatment. Written in such a way, any parent could read and truly learn about the challenges their child might be experiencing. This workbook has a tremendous amount of educational materials for parents, clinicians, educators or anyone working with children and teens who have a sensory processing challenge. The book is a gem, a must have if you have any type of interaction with children and/or teens who experience sensory processing challenges.

- Molly Gratton, LCSW, RPT-S (Owner, Molly and Me Counseling)

Dr. Grant has researched and collaborated with some of the best professionals in the area of sensory processing challenges. This workbook provides a helpful, practical tool to understand and implement meaningful treatment for this childhood developmental disorder. The need for more providers to step into this world is strong. As we learn more about sensory challenges, we are better able to offer differential diagnosing and get kids the help they need. The standards of practice are constantly evolving. Grasping deeper concepts embedded in the neuroscience of development pushes treatment into a world of comprehensive, holistic approaches meant to enrich a child's (and their family's) quality of life. Dr. Grant makes these concepts easier to understand and provides a continuum of tools to help us develop best practices and scientifically rooted treatment plans. Providers, parents, teachers, day care staff, and others will benefit from having this book to help serve as a guide to the develop of a sensory rich environment for children and youth to develop--growing into strong, independent people.

- Dr. Patricia Gilbaugh (Founder and Director, Grace C Mae Advocate Center)

In Understanding Sensory Processing Challenges, Dr. Grant has provided the reader with a roadmap to understanding sensory stages and the unique needs of each step along the way. The workbook format he has chosen allows the reader to understand the basics while learning methods of moving forward toward success. The activities allow the application to a full range of ages. The use of case examples clarifies the applications. In this book, Dr. Grant gives the reader the unique gift of learning to understand how to bridge the gap from theory into practice. The activities incorporate acceptance of the child's diversity, and acknowledge the feelings associated with sensory processing challenges. I would recommend this book to parents, teachers, therapists and counselors who are looking for activities to help this growing population.

- Dr. Linda Barboa (Author, Stars in Her Eyes and the Albert Book Series)

Grant's Understanding Sensory Processing Workbook for Children and Teens fills a large void in the field of child psychotherapy literature. Sensory Processing Disorder (SPD) is a growing challenge that impacts children across the spectrum of cognitive, emotional, and behavioral challenges. It is difficult to change behaviors if a child doesn't know how to regulate their bodies. In this workbook, the neurological, emotional, and behavioral knowledge come together to provide the reader with a coherent, easy to understand guide in helping kids and their parents understand and navigate the child's sensory world. Grant is able to inform the reader of not just the diagnostic issues and challenges children and teens with sensory issues face but offers specific protocols and assessment tools to utilize when working with children and teens who experience sensory struggles. This workbook is full of practical, play-based interventions that can be used across clinical settings. I especially like how Grant involves the parents into the child's treatment and uses them as a resource throughout this book. I would recommend this book to new and seasoned clinicians alike!

- Clair Mellenthin, LCSW, RPT-S (Director of Child & Adolescent Services Wasatch Family Therapy)

Dr Grant has complied this excellent resource for practitioners to assist their clients and families to understand and address the complex needs of individuals with sensory processing disorder. As a professional and parent of a child with significant SPD challenges, the format and exercises included in this workbook will facilitate understanding and practical techniques for everyday use. Dr. Grant's attention to the specifics of each sense so that the client can identify their own sensitivities and ways to regulate themselves is helpful for those families struggling with SPD. SPD is not something someone out grows, it continues to morph and challenge them in various ways as they develop. This book will facilitate a well-rounded approach and guideline to follow when life with SPD gets challenging. Well done Dr. Grant in helping to educate families on Sensory Processing Disorder!

- Cary Hamilton MFT, LMHC, CMHS, RPT-S (Owner, Olympia Therapy)

Dr. Grant has written a highly pragmatic book that not only informs adults and children alike on basic knowledge regarding sensory processing challenges, but also provides easy to use activities that could be helpful for such disorders. Chapters are well organized and follow a logical sequence of first describing and evaluating sensory difficulties, then outlining treatment plans and appropriate activities, followed by ways of seeking feedback from children to hopefully stimulate their insights and the adults understanding of their condition. One of the unique features of this book are the guidelines offered to elicit the feelings from the child clients that are participating in the activities. Hopefully not only do they provide potential for promoting parent/therapists to be more observant, understanding and adaptive to what their children are experiencing and need, but also to create insights for the children in understanding themselves and what they can do to help themselves. I would highly recommend this book for any therapists working with clients having sensory processing difficulties.

- Dr. Evangeline Munns (Clinical Psychologist, Theraplay Supervisor and Trainer)

This book provides insight for those working with children presenting with sensory processing challenges. A very exciting source of information and activities to add to the practitioner's tool kit. It has a very good overview of what a practitioner needs to know to really understand and help these children and their families who are affected by sensory processing struggles.

- Audrey Gregan Modikoane CPT-S, Dip Ed Froebel, Dip Sp Ed (Owner, Garden Play Therapy Centre)

Wow, thank you Robert Jason Grant for creating a book that every therapist and teacher should have to assist children struggling with sensory challenges. As a child therapist, I also plan on recommending this book to the families I work with. This is such an important topic for people to understand and the activities included are simple yet effective. This book is a gem that needed to be written.

- Tammi Van Hollander LCSW, RPT (Owner, Main Line Play Therapy)

Thank You

My family

My friends

My play therapy community

The reviewers and contributors to this book – Amy Vaughan, Cary Hamilton, Mistie Barnes, Tracy Turner-Bumberry, Evangeline Munns, Patricia Gilbaugh, Clair Mellenthin, Tammi Van Hollander, Kim Vander Dussen, Molly Gratton, Audrey Gregan Modikoane, and Linda Barboa.

My editor – Valerie Turner

My clients

My autism community

My inspirations

My God

Contents

Understanding Sensory Processing Challenges

A Workbook for Children and Teens

About Sensory Processing

Many children and teens experience sensory processing challenges and/or have a diagnosis of sensory processing disorder. Terms related to sensory challenges include sensory integration dysfunction, sensory modulation disorder, sensory based motor disorder, and sensory discrimination disorder. This workbook is not intended to be an in-depth examination of sensory issues and disorders. It is intended to present a more generalized overview of sensory challenges to help guide the practitioner or parent in working with children and teens to help explain sensory issues. Practitioners/parents are encouraged to learn more about sensory issues (a guide at the end of the workbook provides several resources) and consult with an occupational therapist trained in sensory processing therapy.

Children and teens experience the world around them through their senses, constantly receiving stimuli and processing through one or more of the eight sensory areas. The typical child can accurately perceive, process, and respond to the myriad of stimuli in his or her environment, focusing on important stimuli, such as someone's voice, and filtering out unimportant stimuli, such as a truck driving past. For children who struggle with sensory processing, the same environment and accompanying stimuli can be uncomfortable, overwhelming, and even frightening (Goodman-Scott & Lambert, 2015).

Sensory processing refers to the way the nervous system receives messages from the senses and turns them into responses. For those with sensory challenges, sensory information goes into the brain but does not get organized into appropriate responses. Those with sensory challenges perceive and/or respond to sensory information differently than most other people. Unlike people who have impaired sight or hearing, those with sensory struggles do detect the sensory information; however, the sensory information gets "mixed up" in their brain and, therefore, the responses are inappropriate in the context in which they find themselves (STAR Institute 2017, www.spdstar.org)

Ayres (1991) stated that sensory integration dysfunction relates to the brain not processing or organizing the flow of sensory input in a manner that gives individuals meaningful, precise information about themselves and their world. Sensory processing challenges resemble a neurological "traffic jam" that prevents certain parts of the brain from receiving the information needed to interpret sensory information correctly. It is a condition that exists when sensory signals do not get organized into appropriate responses. When the brain is not processing sensory input well, it is usually not directing behavior well, which can lead to a myriad of unwanted behavior reactions and responses. When there is poor sensory regulation, learning is difficult for the individual, and the individual typically feels uncomfortable about himself or herself and cannot easily cope with ordinary demands and stress.

A child or teen with sensory processing issues finds it difficult to process and act upon information received through the senses, which creates challenges in performing countless everyday tasks. Motor clumsiness, behavioral problems, anxiety, depression, and school failure can accompany sensory processing struggles (Sensory Processing Disorder Foundation, 2016). Children and adolescents with sensory processing challenges may have struggles in most or all areas of their life. Along with sensory integration struggles, a child may also experience frustration, rejection from peers, academic struggles, self-esteem struggles, mislabeled and misunderstood behaviors, and emotional regulation challenges. Sensory processing challenges should be viewed as a spectrum of presentation with individual challenges and strengths - each child or teen with sensory issues will be affected differently.

Sensory processing challenges often lead to problematic or unwanted behaviors. Often the problematic behavior is a coping skill or reaction to the sensory challenge that is happening within the child. Vaughan (2014) stated that for some, sensory processing challenges will present as defiant behavior, opposition, or refusal to cooperate. These behaviors may develop out of a need to avoid or escape a challenging situation. When children present with sensory created behaviors, it is often the problematic behavior that gets attention and the problematic behavior that gets addressed, while the root issue of the sensory challenge is ignored.

Although the manifestation and effect of sensory challenges can look different for each child or teen, Miller (2014) proposed some fundamental elements regarding sensory processing disorder:

1. Sensory processing disorder (SPD) is a complex disorder of the brain that affects developing children and adults.

2. Parent surveys, clinical assessments, and laboratory protocols exist to identify children with SPD.

3. At least one in twenty people in the general population may be affected by SPD.

4. In children who are gifted and those with ADHD, autism, and fragile X syndrome, the prevalence of SPD is much higher than in the general population.

5. Studies have found a significant difference between the physiology of children with SPD and children who are typically developing.

6. Studies have found a significant difference between the physiology of children with SPD and children with ADHD.

7. Those with SPD have unique sensory symptoms that are not explained by other known disorders.

8. Heredity may be one cause of the disorder.

9. Laboratory studies suggest that the sympathetic and parasympathetic nervous systems are not functioning typically in children with SPD.

10. Preliminary research data support decades of anecdotal evidence that occupational therapy is an effective intervention for treating the symptoms of SPD.

Vaughan (2014) proposed that sensory development happens in four stages. The first stage is awareness of the environment. This stage involves the ability to gather accurate information, as well as enough information about the environment around us. We begin to use this information to work for us and understand that we can change things and make things happen. The second stage is self-regulation. This stage involves learning to regulate ourselves and our responses. We begin to modulate our emotions. The third stage is controlled response. This stage involves learning to control our responses. We can choose not to respond or how we will respond. This stage is where sensory strengths and challenges begin to be noticed. The final stage is skilled response. This stage involves being able to take in information, keep it in the appropriate context, and respond successfully.

Sensory processing challenges affect not only the individual child but the whole family and extend into all the environments in which the child participates. A child's or teen's sensory struggles may be confined to one sensory area, or he or she may struggle with multiple sensory areas or in the simultaneous integration of multiple sensory areas. The degree of struggle will be unique to each child, and how each child and teen perceives and uses sensory input will vary. To fully understand sensory processing and the variations in how different people react to sensory input, it is important to understand each sensory area and how individuals can be over or under responsive in regard to sensory challenges. Professionals and parents will want to gain a thorough understanding of sensory challenges and learn effective strategies and interventions to help children and teens with sensory struggles make improvement gains.

The Eight Sensory Areas

Biel (2014) stated that sensory areas pick up detailed messages from the environment and information from within our own bodies. Working together, these senses integrate seamlessly to tell us what is going on around us and what we should do at any given time, giving us an accurate, reliable sense of ourselves and our place in the world.

1. **Visual** *(sight)* – The visual system detects information through our eyes and then interprets or makes sense of that information in the brain. In addition to how clearly our eyes register images, our eye muscles play a significant role in how well we control our gaze to adjust to movement, shift our focus, and how we use both of our eyes together. Children and teens with visual sense challenges may have extreme sensitivity to light, have difficulty maintaining eye contact, difficulty maintaining their focus on something, difficulty reading, complain of headaches, rub their eyes, and squint often. They may also have difficulty with hand writing, bump into things, and become easily distracted by visual stimuli. Activities that stimulate the visual sense include visual tracking games, hidden picture games, throwing and catching a ball, matching and sorting games, memory games, blowing and popping bubbles, and practicing eye contact.

2. **Auditory** *(sound)* – The auditory system includes hearing, listening, and being able to filter and selectively attend to auditory stimuli. Children and teens with auditory sense struggles may experience certain sounds, tones, and levels of noise as painful and distracting. They may cover their ears, refuse to participate in activities or programs that incorporate unpleasant sounds, try to get away from noise, recognize sounds that others cannot hear, or display a variety of unwanted behavior responses. They may also seek out certain tones or types of sound for sensory input. Activities that stimulate the auditory sense include playing games that involve exposure to various sounds such as musical instruments, bells, and signing bowls. Exposure sounds should begin with softer and more pleasant sounds.

3. **Olfactory** *(smell)* – The olfactory bulb is in the most forward part of the brain on the bottom side of the brain. The olfactory bulb transmits smell information from the nose to the brain and is thus necessary for a proper sense of smell. (Star Institute, 2018 www.spdstar.org). Children and teens with olfactory sense struggles may experience strong negative reactions to unpleasant smells and notice smells that others do not. They may also frequently smell objects and people seeking sensory input. Activities that stimulate the olfactory sense include playing games experimenting with different odors (starting with weaker and

generally more pleasant odors) such as scratch and sniff stickers, a nature walk, scented play dough and markers.

4. **Gustatory** *(taste)* – Gustatory is our sense of taste, it allows us to recognize the five basic taste sensations of sweet, sour, salty, bitter, and umami. This sense is meant to keep us safe from ingesting things that are toxic, spoiled, or inedible. Children and teens over or under responding to oral input, may display a range of disruptive behaviors including picky eating, limits in the taste texture, or temperature of food that will be eaten, dislike brushing teeth and going to the dentist, frequent drooling, and chewing on objects such as pencils, toys, and clothing. Activities that stimulate the gustatory sense include eating foods that are crunchy, utilizing an appropriate chew toy, and playing games that require blowing – bubbles, balloons, musical instruments.

5. **Tactile** *(touch)* – The tactile system is extremely important in sensory processing. Many individuals with sensory struggles have tactile symptoms such as tactile defensiveness or under-responsivity to touch and pain. The touch system is one of the three foundational systems used in sensory integration treatment (Star Institute, 2018 www.spdstar.org) The sense of touch is the activation of neural receptors generally in the skin. The sense of touch encompasses many different types of stimuli including but not limited to pain, pressure, tension, temperature, texture, shape, weight, contours and vibrations. Children and teens with touch sensory struggles may dislike wearing certain clothing, dislike washing their hands, having their hair cut or washed, taking a shower, brushing their teeth or being touched by others. They may also overly touch other people or things and not understand their own strength. Activities that stimulate touch sense include playing with fidget and sensory toys, playing in sand, water, and other sensory trays, and manipulating various tactile objects.

6. **Vestibular** – The vestibular system contributes to balance and orientation in space. It is the leading system informing us about movement and position of head relative to gravity. Our movements include two positions: rotations and linear directionality. Thus, the vestibular system has two related components: the semicircular canal system - related to detecting rotation and the otoliths - related to detecting linear acceleration/deceleration (Star Institute, 2018 www.spdstar.org). It is responsible for informing us whether our body is stationary or moving, how fast it is moving, and in what direction. Children and teens who experience vestibular struggles may have difficulty with activities where their feet leave the ground, may lay or slouch instead of sitting, be impulsive, clumsy, or move with extreme caution. They may also prefer sedentary activities and often experience motion sickness. Activities that stimulate the vestibular sense include swinging, hanging upside down, running,

jumping, skipping, sliding, rolling down a hill, going through an obstacle course, and jumping on a trampoline.

7. **Proprioceptive** – The proprioceptive system senses the position, location, orientation, and movement of the body muscles and joints. Proprioception provides us with the sense of the relative position of neighboring parts of the body and effort used to move body parts. The proprioceptive sense combines sensory information from neurons in the inner ear (detecting motion and orientation) and stretch receptors in the muscles and the joint-supporting ligaments for stance (Star Institute, 2018 www.spdstar.org). The proprioceptive system is our body's ability to sense where we are in relationship to our surroundings and our other body parts. Children and teens who experience proprioceptive struggles may be frequently crashing or bumping into things, falling, frequently climbing and jumping, enjoy deep pressure, apply too much force in writing or coloring, play too rough, may not recognize the amount of force they are exerting, and often kick or stomp their feet. Activities that stimulate the proprioceptive sense include punching, pulling, climbing, crawling, lifting, squeezing, and stretching.

8. **Interoception** – Interoception refers to sensations related to the physiological/physical condition of the body. Interoceptors are internal sensors that provide a sense of what our internal organs are feeling. Interoception detects responses that guide regulation, including hunger, thirst, heart rate, respiration, and elimination (Star Institute, 2018 www.spdstar). Interoception works with the vestibular and proprioceptive senses to determine how an individual perceives his or her own body. Interoception is associated with autonomic motor control and is different than mechano-reception (in the skin) and proprioception (in the muscles and joints). Interoception helps you feel and understand what is going on inside your body. Interoception experiences include internal pain, temperature, itch, hunger, thirst, bladder needs, and the need for air. Children and teens with interoception struggles may have difficulty "feeling" their emotions. They may not understand the cues their body is providing that help them interpret an emotion. They may not recognize when they are hungry or full, need to go to the bathroom, or are experiencing an internal pain. Interoceptive struggles may be improved by implementing proprioceptive and vestibular activities and implementing behavioral strategies designed to help children better identify internal issues and needs.

Over and Under Responsivity

Children who struggle with sensory processing challenges can be over responsive (hypersensitive) or under responsive (hyposensitive) in their sensory processing. It is possible for a child to be both under and over responsive. This can be present in one sensory area or multiple sensory areas. Typically, more than one sensory area is affected by over or under responsiveness. Over responsive or hypersensitive children tend to over respond to or are highly sensitive to incoming sensory information. These children may overreact to situations such as screaming when lightly touched or needing to wear dark glasses in normal light. Under responsive or hyposensitive children tend to under react to incoming sensory information. These children may not notice pain and may be prone to unsafe behaviors and actions. They may also seek sensory information such as humming or singing to gain auditory input.

Case Example: Molly (Over Responsive), a 13-year-old girl, entered therapy with a diagnosis of ASD and sensory processing challenges. Molly was over responsive in auditory, tactile, and vestibular sensory areas. She would often sing and hum to seek auditory input. Molly struggled with many types of clothing and would wear only certain fabrics that fit her in a specific way. She also struggled to stay in one spot, often bouncing on an exercise ball, lying on the floor, and flopping around on various pieces of furniture.

Case Example: Sam (Under Responsive), a 7-year-old male, entered therapy with a diagnosis of ASD and sensory processing challenges. Sam was under responsive in multiple sensory areas, but his most challenging area was tactile. Sam would often seek tactile experiences, needing to touch everything and change his seating options regularly. Sam often engaged in unsafe behaviors such as catching small wild animals (skunks, squirrels, rabbits) with his bare hands. When he would catch an animal, it would bite him repeatedly, but Sam appeared to be unaware of the pain.

Over Responsive Signs: frequently covers hears, running away, avoiding touch, extremely distracted, picky eater, gaging, overreacting to smells, fearful, wants to wear sunglasses all the time, dislikes fast movements and playground equipment, poor fine motor skills, fatigues easily, and poor gross motor skills.

Under Responsive Signs: frequently touching and smelling objects and people, attracted to certain lights or sounds, likes feeling enclosed or wrapped up, may not respond to auditory instructions, ignores unpleasant sounds or odors, moves slowly or appears lethargic, trouble waking in the mornings, difficulty getting started on tasks, and does not notice touching or being touched by others.

Causes and Diagnosis

The exact cause of Sensory Processing Disorder (SPD) has not yet been identified. Preliminary studies and research suggest that SPD is often inherited. Prenatal and birth complications, as well as certain environmental factors, have also been implicated as causal in SPD. Research continues to be implemented to determine the causes of Sensory Processing Disorder.

Many different professionals through formal and informal processes may discover that a child or teen has sensory challenges. A formal diagnosis of Sensory Processing Disorder is typically given by an occupational therapist trained in evaluating sensory processing. Early identification, diagnosis, and treatment produces the best outcomes for helping children with SPD improve. Occupational therapists use a variety of measures to diagnose SPD. They may incorporate clinical interviews, observations, questionnaires, and standardized testing. The Sensory Profile 2 and the Sensory Integration and Praxis Tests are two commonly used instruments to provide diagnosis.

Professionals and parents may want to implement a screening process before referring for a formal evaluation. A screening process does not provide a diagnosis but helps to establish if some sensory struggles may need further evaluation. A screening process could include observing the child, noting and documenting what appears to be sensory issues, and completing screening checklists. A list of some sensory screening tools is provided:

- *Sensory Symptoms Checklist* – www.spdstar.org/basic/symptoms-checklist
- *SPD Checklist* – www.developmentalpathways.com/services-sensory.html
- *SPD Symptoms Checklist* – www.spdsupport.org/resources/symptoms.shtml
- *Sensory Home Screening Tool* – www.sensoryprocessingchallenges.com
- *Sensory School Screening Tool* – www.sensoryprocessingchallenges.com

Sensory processing challenges are known to co-occur with other issues and disorders. Among the most common disorders that can accompany sensory processing challenges are autism spectrum disorder, attention-deficit hyperactivity disorder, language disorders, learning disabilities, post-traumatic stress disorder, and fragile X syndrome. The Sensory Processing Disorder Foundation (2018) claims that as many as 1 in every 20 people—both children and adults—in the United States is affected by sensory processing challenges. Currently, sensory processing challenges appear worse in children. Evidence suggests that sensory struggles tend to get better with neurological maturation. Many people learn to understand their struggles and gain coping strategies better as they grow. Adults with sensory challenges seem to have a greater ability to manage the struggles and the environment.

Sensory Processing Challenges

The STAR Institute (2017) defined Sensory Processing Disorder or SPD (originally called Sensory Integration Dysfunction) as a neurological disorder in which the sensory information that the individual perceives results in abnormal responses. A more formal definition is the following: SPD is a neurophysiologic condition in which sensory input either from the environment or from one's body is poorly detected, modulated, or interpreted and/or to which atypical responses are observed. Individuals may be evaluated for a sensory processing disorder and formally given the diagnosis.

Some individuals may not be formally diagnosed with sensory processing disorder or meet the full criteria for diagnosis yet struggle with sensory processing. Children with autism and related conditions often struggle with sensory processing despite not having a formal diagnosis of sensory processing disorder. It is likely that sensory processing disorder is underdiagnosed. Without a thorough understand of sensory processing, it would be typical to label the sensory-related signs and symptoms as something else and be unaware of how sensory struggles can manifest.

It is important for practitioners and parents to be familiar with the signs and symptoms of sensory processing struggles. The following list presents some common symptoms:

- withdraws when touched
- is easily fatigued
- struggles with interacting with peers
- dislikes dirt or other substance on hands
- complains about the texture or temperature of certain foods
- has high or low tolerance to pain
- refuses to eat certain foods
- exhibits behavioral problems
- elopes from various environments

- avoids creative or messy play
- may appear fidgety or needing to change body position often
- displays clumsiness, poor fine motor control
- has difficulty self-calming
- is sensitive to tags in clothing
- struggles with dysregulation
- experiences challenges with body balance and other movements
- is unaware of dangerous actions

- complains about irritants in their environment
- demonstrates avoidance behaviors
- has handwriting challenges
- is oversensitive to sounds, light, or certain smells
- plays too rough; lacks understanding of how hard or soft they are touching others
- is unaware of internal states such as pain, hunger, and bowl movements
- is hypersensitive to certain fabric

Treatment

The most appropriate treatment for sensory processing challenges is occupational therapy with a focus on sensory processing. Research also indicates that early intervention produces the best outcomes (Kranowitz, 2005; Delaney, 2008). Occupational therapists work in many different settings and are often contracted with schools to provide services in the school setting. Practitioners/parents with concerns about sensory processing challenges should refer to an occupational therapist for a complete sensory evaluation and follow-up treatment. Practitioners/parents may work in collaboration with the occupational therapist.

Other treatments that may be implemented for children with sensory challenges include the following: play therapy, physical therapy, speech and language therapy, music therapy, ABA services, vision therapy, listening therapy, and chiropractic services. Parents may also provide valuable intervention for their child with sensory processing challenges by becoming educated about their child's sensory issues and learning techniques to help their child improve his or her sensory processing ability. Treatment may also involve assistive devices such as sound blocking headphones, light blocking glasses, gloves or special clothing, special seating, and selective foods that may be a part of the child's daily functioning.

Some individuals with sensory challenges have found that pairing therapy with alternative treatments such as acupuncture helps to alleviate struggles. Brushing, or the Wilbarger protocol, and craniosacral manipulation have also been reported to be helpful as complementary therapies for some individuals. It should be noted that research has not confirmed the effectiveness of holistic and alternative approaches. Any alternative treatment should be administered under the supervision of a qualified therapist.

Treatments for sensory processing challenges should clearly define what the treatment can and will address and how the treatment helps children with sensory challenges. Treatments should also have a process for evaluating to ensure that progress toward treatment goals are being met. Treatments should be affordable and accessible, and work with the child and family and not create an additional stressor for the child or family. Standard treatments for sensory processing challenges often use the principles of the theory of neuroplasticity, which contends that the brain can change based on experience. Professionals and parents should invest time in researching any treatment that promotes being beneficial for children with sensory challenges and critically evaluate the potential benefits and or harm in participating in the promoted treatment.

Sensory Diet

Credited with creating the term *sensory diet*, Patricia Wilbarger (Wilbarger, 1984) described the concept as a form of home program intervention plan that incorporates organizing sensory input, or utilizes already existing sensory input, into everyday life to assist the person to maintain a regulated behavioral state, such as the calm, alert state required to participate in certain environments. Sensory diet strategies may be implemented at regular intervals throughout the day. These strategies may be performed prior to times considered challenging, to prepare or set up the body to maintain an organized state throughout the activity. They also may be used during activities to assist the client to maintain an organized state throughout the activity.

A sensory diet will look different for each child and be designed individually to meet specific goals for the target child. Biel (2014) talked about a sensory diet or sensory program as a personalized schedule of activities that help a child feel satisfied throughout the day. The goal is to give the child the correct type of sensory input in regular, controlled doses so there is no need to resort to unwanted behaviors because the child's sensory needs are being met. A sensory diet must be tailored to each child's specific sensory needs and may include many strategies implemented by the child or by others who are assisting the child.

Dorman, Lehsten, Woodin, Cohen, Schweitzer, & Tona (2009) described a sensory diet as each person having unique sensory preferences and needs and establishing individual sensory strategies, as strategies would affect each person differently. Some real-life examples for how to address sensory preferences or needs include taking a walk when feeling the need to move around, chewing gum or licorice sticks as alternatives to nail biting when anxious and taking deep breaths when feeling anger building. A more formal example might be for a child who has been determined as having proprioceptive sensory challenges—this child might have a list of activities to complete such as doing wall pushups, doing some marching and running games, jumping on a trampoline, and climbing stairs.

A sensory diet is typically created and implemented by an occupational therapist who has thoroughly evaluated the child to determine his or her sensory needs and challenges. The occupational therapist creates a list of activities that the child can complete throughout his or her day to address the sensory needs and challenges. The occupational therapist may teach others in the child's life (parents, school personnel, other professionals) the activities and how to implement the activities with the child. Many book and web resources are available to practitioners and parents regarding sensory diets. It is recommended that practitioners and parents work with or at least consult with an occupational therapist before implementing any form of sensory diet.

Sensory Processing and Play

Ayres (1991) reported that the importance of play in sensory processing is highly underrated. The essential ingredient in play is the child's expression of his or her inner drive toward self-fulfillment as a sensory-motor being. Through play, the child obtains the sensory input from his or her body and from gravity that is essential for both motor and emotional development. Running, turning, bending, touching things, pushing, pulling, rolling, crawling, climbing, jumping, and so on produce a tremendous amount of vestibular, proprioceptive, and tactile input. The more varied the play, the more it contributes to development.

Cross (2010) proposed that children and teens learn when they use their senses during play. The organization or sensory integration allows controlled sensory input, which influences a child's learning potential and response to the environment. There are eight senses of sensory integration: tactile, visual, auditory, olfactory, gustatory, proprioceptive, vestibular, and interoceptive. When the sensory areas are aligned with appropriate strategies and techniques, this can produce increased adaptive behaviors, positive response to motor issues, and creative connections to play. Sensory processing play should be uniquely tailored to the individual child, should stimulate the child's interests, and should consider the child's distinct play preferences. Children who are offered play experiences that are intentionally planned with the eight sensory areas in mind can make gains in sensory struggles and function better in their world.

Brady, Gonzalez, Zawadzki, & Presley (2011) proposed that children engage in play through games, manipulation of toys, interacting with peers, and art and expressive materials. Play is often used as the main modality in therapy with children as it captures the child's attention and creates a positive experience for the child. Play therapy is a type of mental health treatment that utilizes the therapeutic powers of play to help children and teens process, heal, and manage a variety of diagnoses and life adjustment issues. Play therapy provides the opportunity to help children with sensory processing challenges develop coping skills, improve self-esteem, improve social skills, reduce anxiety levels, provide bibliotherapy, and help children understand their disorder.

Play therapy also provides a systemic approach, working with family members and other adults in the child's environments. Play therapists typically utilize toys, art materials, expressive materials, games, music, and movement to address issues that children with sensory challenges struggle with. Additionally, play therapists can provide sensory input through sand trays, water trays, putty, movement games, etc., that help support the sensory diet offered by the occupational therapist. Often, play therapists implement a sensory play diet that is taught to parents to use at home to help their child gain regulation ability.

Sensory Play Diet

Children and teens with sensory processing challenges benefit from participating in a consistent regiment of activities and tasks designed to improve sensory struggle areas. As defined previously, a sensory diet is a program intervention plan that addresses sensory challenges through specific activities and interventions that are incorporated into a child's everyday life. A sensory play diet builds upon the constructs of a sensory diet by mindfully incorporating play (the natural language of children) to enhance the sensory processing experience and cultivate the therapeutic powers of play.

Schaefer (2014) described the therapeutic powers of play as the specific change agents in which play initiates, facilitates, or strengthens their therapeutic effect. The play helps produce the change and is not just a medium for applying other change agents; nor does it just moderate the strengths or direction of the therapeutic change. Twenty core agents of change have been identified in the therapeutic powers of play: self-expression, access to the unconscious, direct teaching, indirect teaching, catharsis, abreaction, counterconditioning fears, stress inoculation, stress management, therapeutic relationship, attachment, social competence, empathy, creative problem solving, moral development, accelerated psychological development, self-regulation, and self-esteem. When children can access the therapeutic powers of play, they move from a singular solution focus to a holistic, sustainable gain in understanding and addressing their own sensory processing challenges.

When we understand the sensory issues a child is dealing with, we can use play to not only address the challenges of living with a brain that processes signals from the body differently but also to help with additional regulation and communication struggles that are often present with children who have sensory processing challenges. Introducing play therapy interventions encourages the brain to work more effectively at processing sensory input and vestibular information. Play is therefore vital for the healthy development of the body and the brain. Play therapy interventions provide children with safe and engaging opportunity to experience sensory input (Moor, 2008).

Play is the foundation of a sensory play diet, harnessing the therapeutic powers of play to affect a sustainable change for the child with sensory challenges. Pragmatically speaking, play incorporation into the sensory diet experience brings an engagement and enjoyment process to the protocol, which promotes greater participation, cooperation, and repetition of the daily sensory interventions. Children desire to play, and they are more likely to engage and participate in sensory interventions that are play-based and enjoyable. The more the child participates, the more he or she will make progress toward improving the sensory processing challenges. The following guide outlines the steps for implementing a sensory play diet:

1. The practitioner or parent should have a thorough assessment of the sensory processing challenges the child is experiencing. This may be in the form of a previous sensory evaluation or a history of assessment provided by the parent. This might also mean a referral to an occupational therapist to conduct a sensory evaluation. Regardless of the process, the practitioner or parent should have a clear understanding of what the child's sensory struggles are and how the struggles are affecting the child.

2. The practitioner or parent should have a thorough assessment of the child's play interests. This can be done formally or informally. A formal play assessment can be facilitated by a play therapist to indicate the areas of play the child participates in the most, or a preference assessment can be conducted to note the types of toys and materials the child is most drawn toward. Informally, the practitioner or parent can observe the child's play and note what he or she likes and seems to enjoy doing the most. Many children and teens will be able to indicate what they like and do not like and may even participate in establishing the sensory play diet.

3. The third step is selecting the play therapy interventions to address the sensory challenges. Once an assessment of the child's sensory struggles and his or her play interests have been identified, the practitioner or parent can choose play therapy interventions to implement with the child or teen to help address the specific sensory challenges. The practitioner or parent will also make note of any materials that are needed for the play therapy interventions and have those materials available to use. This workbook highlights several play therapy interventions that can be used to help address sensory challenges. Additional resources for play therapy interventions can be found in the references and resources section of this workbook.

4. Once the play therapy interventions have been selected, the practitioner or parent should organize the sensory play diet into a formal program. An example of a formal sensory play diet is found in the resources section of this workbook. The program should include the location (office, home, school, other) where the sensory play is going to happen. If there is more than one location, this should be noted. It should also be noted if there will be a designated space in the location where the sensory play diet will take place.

    The program should also include when and how often the child or teen will participate in the sensory play interventions. This could be daily, every other day, or once a week. The length of time the child will engage in the sensory play diet interventions will also be established: 10 minutes, 20 minutes, or 30 minutes? The length should be determined based on the child's age, developmental ability, and the child's circumstance. For example, a child participating in a sensory play diet in a school setting likely will not be able to participate for 30 minutes but may be able to have a 10-minute sensory play break.

The practitioner or parent will need to indicate if someone will be working with the child, assisting the child to complete the interventions, or if the child will be engaging in all or some of the sensory play diet activities on his or her own, without assistance. If a person will be working with the child, it should be established ahead of time who this person will be, and the child should be aware that this person will be working with them. It is likely that most children will begin with needed assistance from another person and then work into doing more play interventions on their own. It should be noted that some play therapy interventions require another person to complete. If the practitioner or parent is trying to have the child engage in a sensory play diet without assistance, the practitioner or parent should avoid play interventions that require more than one person.

5. Lastly, the practitioner or parent will have an introductory time with the child or teen and explain what they will be doing and when they will be going it. The child should understand that he or she will be participating in the sensory play diet, what the expectations are, and who will be working with them. The practitioner or parent should periodically evaluate the program to make sure it is effective in helping the child improve his or her sensory processing challenges. All elements of the sensory play diet can be modified as needed.

When implementing play therapy interventions for sensory processing challenges, a variety of toys and materials are available to use. A child should never be forced to participate in an activity or intervention or forced to use a certain toy or material that he or she does not want to use. It is beneficial to understand what toys and materials the child might have a sensitivity toward and what toys and materials the child might be naturally drawn toward. Using toys and materials the child is naturally drawn toward will produce better outcomes in play therapy sensory work. Some typical toys found in a play therapy room that might be beneficial in sensory work include playdough, clay, putty, sand trays, water trays, exercise balls, fidget toys, movement games, finger paints, bop bags, music instruments, art materials, Legos, blocks, sensory balls, bean bag chairs, and various tactile manipulatives.

How to Use This Workbook

Children and teens with sensory processing challenges may have a myriad of issues that need to be addressed. One central issue that is often neglected is helping children and teens with sensory processing challenges to understand their disorder. Many children lack an appropriate awareness of how sensory processing affects them, and they lack the ability to process their thoughts and emotions regarding having a sensory disorder.

This workbook is designed to assist both practitioners and parents in helping children and teens understand and process their thoughts and emotions about having sensory processing challenges. Practitioners/parents are encouraged to learn more about sensory processing disorder. The resources section of this workbook lists several books, websites, apps, and games that can help practitioners/parents gain more insight about sensory processing and provide additional tools to help children and adolescents learn more about the diagnosis.

This workbook is designed to help children who have sensory processing challenges learn about their disorder. Practitioners/parents are encouraged to use this workbook to assist their child in learning about how sensory processing struggles affect him or her. Parents can also share this workbook with family members and other individuals such as school staff, recreational workers, church staff, etc., who interact regularly with their child to help these individuals better understand a child with sensory challenges.

The workbook can be completed by starting at the beginning and going through each worksheet with the child, or each worksheet can be targeted separately as an individual concept to explain and explore with the child. The worksheets provide an opportunity for the child to share his or her thoughts and questions. Each worksheet also provides the opportunity for practitioners/parents to answer the child's questions and further explain the concepts related to sensory processing.

Although many practitioners/parents are well educated about sensory processing, additional information is presented to aid practitioners/parents in presenting and processing each worksheet page/topic. Each worksheet begins with suggestions regarding how to use each worksheet page and information that can be shared and discussed for optimal results.

The Worksheets

This Workbook Is about Understanding Sensory Processing Challenges

Using and processing the worksheet

Children and teens who struggle with sensory processing challenges may have difficulty understanding what sensory challenges are and how the challenges affect their life. This worksheet asks the child or teen to draw a picture of something that feels calm. It will help the practitioner/parent discover if the child or teen can identify the feeling of calm (some children may not be able to do this). It will also help the practitioner/parent understand what feels calming to the child, as the child may need to practice calming strategies to help address sensory challenges.

If the child does not want to draw, he or she can talk about something that feels calm. The child can also draw or talk about multiple things that feel calm if he or she can identify more than one thing. If the child identifies calming activities that can be practiced, the practitioner/parent should take time to role play or practice some of the calming strategies. It is important to introduce this workbook in a positive manner. It is best if the child or teen can feel encouraged about completing the worksheets. The practitioner/parent is free to add any playful or engaging elements to this workbook, especially if it would help the child feel more comfortable or increase participation.

Let's start by drawing in the picture below something that feels calm to you.

What Do You Know about Sensory Processing Challenges?

Using and processing the worksheet

This worksheet asks the child or teen to write or talk about what he or she currently understands about sensory processing challenges. It will be helpful to the practitioner/parent to understand what the child or teen thinks about sensory challenges. This worksheet serves as an assessment piece that focuses on the level of awareness the child currently possesses. It assists the practitioner/parent in better formulating what areas need to be addressed with the child, what misconceptions need to be explained, and what understanding about sensory challenges need to be further developed.

It is likely that some children will not think of anything to write or talk about. The practitioner/parent should simply note this on the worksheet and assume the child is beginning with little to no understanding about sensory processing challenges. At this point, the practitioner/parent can move forward with helping the child or teen understand sensory processing challenges and specifically how the child or teen is affected by sensory challenges.

What do you know about sensory processing challenges?

Write or talk about what you know.

_____

_____

_____

_____

_____

_____

_____

_____

_____

_____

_____

_____

_____

Sensory Processing Activity: I Sense Story

Activity: I Sense Story (by Robert Jason Grant, Ed.D, LPC, RPT-S, ACAS)
Sensory Target Area(s): Visual, Auditory, Tactile, Taste, Olfactory, Proprioceptive, Vestibular
Level: Child and Teen
Modality: Individual, Family, Group
Materials Needed: Paper, Pencil, Various Toys

Introduction

I Sense Story helps children identify and practice working on sensory processing challenges in an engaging and play-based way that promotes relationship development, coping skills, and sensory regulation. This activity is designed to engage multiple sensory areas and can be repeated multiple times with a new story each time.

Instructions

1. The practitioner/parent gives the instructions to the child that the child will be writing a poem and creating a visual activity to go with the poem.

2. The poem is a sentence completion based on the eight sensory areas. It is written as follows: Looks like… Sounds like… Smells like… Tastes like… Feels like… Moves like….

3. The child completes each sentence based on a visual or activity in the playroom. An example would be the following: Sounds like a musical instrument. The child would identify a musical instrument in the playroom and complete the line based on identifying the musical instrument.

4. Once the child is finished, he or she reads the poem and performs the activity that goes with each line of the poem. In the example, the child would read, "Sounds like a musical instrument," and the child would play the selected musical instrument while reading the line.

5. The practitioner/parent allows the child to write the whole poem and select an activity for each line of the poem (each sensory area) but offers help only if the child indicates that he or she needs help. The practitioner/parent can join the child and complete the poem/activity together.

Rationale

This intervention is helpful for children and teens who are experiencing dysregulation or anxiety due to sensory processing challenges. When creating the story, the practitioner/parent should be sensitive to specific sensory challenges the child struggles with and may suggest activities to go with each line of the poem that might be helpful for the child to practice or work on, such as "Feels like a back brush" for children who find it calming to be brushed.

I Sense Story Example

- Looks like funny glasses. (Child finds some funny glasses and puts them on while reading this line.)
- Sounds like a musical instrument. (Child finds a musical instrument and plays it while reading this line.)
- Smells like a dry erase marker. (Child gets a dry erase marker and smells it while reading this line.)
- Tastes like a piece of candy. (Child gets a piece of candy and tastes it while reading this line.)
- Feels like sand in the sand tray. (Child puts hands in the sand tray while reading this line.)
- Moves like a monkey. (Child moves around the room like a monkey while reading this line.)

I Sense Story Example

I Sense Story Worksheet

Child's Name_____

Name of Story_____

Looks Like

_____

Sounds Like

_____

Smells Like

_____

Tastes Like

_____

Feels Like

_____

Moves Like

_____

What Are Some of Your Questions about Sensory Processing Challenges?

Using and processing the worksheet

It is helpful to know what questions children and teens may have about sensory processing. Often children overhear information, are provided explanations, or do research on their own and have some knowledge about issues they struggle with. It is important to know what the child's questions are and make sure to address any inaccurate information. This worksheet asks the child or teen to write down any questions they have about sensory processing challenges. The child may write simply "What is sensory processing?" or the child may have many questions. If the child cannot write, he or she can tell the practitioner/parent the questions, and the practitioner/parent can write them down on the worksheet.

The practitioner/parent should try to address each question that the child or teen produces. If the practitioner/parent does not know the answer, the practitioner/parent should tell the child that they will research the question together and find the answer. The more familiar the practitioner/parent is with sensory processing issues, the better equipped he or she will be to answer any questions the child or teen may have. It is likely that some children will not have any questions. If this is the situation, the practitioner/parent may move forward with additional pages in the workbook.

What are some of your questions about sensory processing challenges?

Let's write them on this sheet.

Sensory Processing Activity: Balancing Act

Activity: Balancing Act (by Cary M. Hamilton, M.A. MFT, LMHC, CMHS, RPT-S)
Sensory Target Area(s): Proprioceptive, Vestibular
Level: Child
Modality: Individual
Materials Needed: Bop Bag, Floor Space

Introduction

This activity involves using a bop bag. These types of bags are commonplace in most play therapy rooms, as they provide a safe way for a child to release his or her anger, aggression, and energy. Bop bags are weighted at the bottom, which allows them to pop back upright after a child knocks it over. Bop bags can be used in many ways, and this activity highlights one way to structure a bop bag activity to improve sensory processing issues.

Instructions

1. The practitioner/parent explains to the child that he or she will be doing an activity to strengthen the muscles and release tension in his or her bodies.

2. The practitioner/parent explains that the child will be using a bop bag and clears a large space in the room (large enough for the bop bag to tip over).

3. The practitioner/parent encourages the child to hit, punch, or kick the bop bag X number of times (the number of times can reflect the child's age or be increased/decreased based on the child's need for sensory input). The child can continue to hit, punch, or kick the bop bag until he or she is no longer interested.

4. The practitioner/parent then encourages the child to run at the bop bag to knock it down. Once the bop bag is on the floor, the child is encouraged to get on the bop bag and find his or her balance on the bag, so the child does not roll off onto the floor. The child can repeat the running, knocking down, and finding his or her balance portion of this activity any number of times until balance is achieved.

Rationale

Children with sensory processing challenges often struggle with core stability, which helps our bodies with gross motor skills, fine motor skills, balance, and coordination of movement. Balancing tasks are a great way to help a child work on building his or her core stability while achieving a goal. A bop bag is typically used to release challenging emotions and aggression; using a bop bag in this way also works on a child's proprioceptive sense, which focuses on the movement of one's muscles and joints. Adding the balance component is an easy way to incorporate both sensory target areas.

Practitioners/parents may find this activity useful with children who arrive to a session dysregulated, or are frequently seeking sensory input from climbing, jumping, and using the bop bag as a tool to meet these needs. Parents can easily purchase a bop bag to have at home for the child to use whenever he or she needs regulation work, or parents can structure time with the bop bag such as implementing this *Balancing Act* activity.

Balancing Act Example

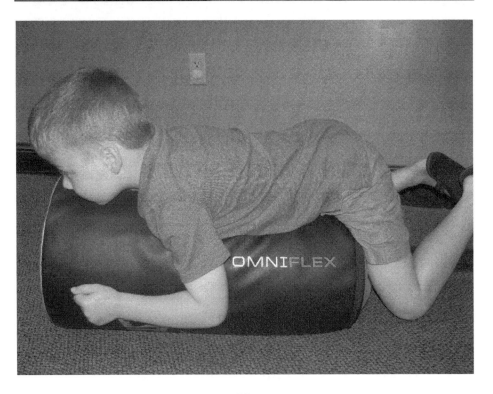

There Are Eight Senses That We Experience

Using and processing the worksheet

This worksheet presents the eight sensory processing areas. There is a list of twelve different things on the worksheet, and the child or teen is asked to circle the eight that represent the eight sensory areas. This worksheet is meant to be a fun guessing activity and should be presented this way. Most children will not be able to identify all eight of the sensory areas. Once the child has circled eight items, the practitioner/parent should celebrate all the correct guesses and indicate to the child the areas that he or she missed. The correct responses are visual, auditory, smell, taste, tactile, vestibular, proprioceptive, and interoceptive.

The practitioner/parent can explain to the child or teen that his or her body is made up of these eight sensory processing areas. The practitioner/parent can give a simple example of one or two of the areas, such as explaining when the child smells something that makes him or her uncomfortable, the child holds his or her nose. Taking in smell through the smell or olfactory sensory processing in the body will feel pleasant, unpleasant, or possibly neutral. This worksheet is an introductory worksheet to the eight sensory processing areas that are explored in more detail in later worksheets.

There are eight senses that we experience.

Circle below what you believe are the eight sensory areas.

Visual

Mechanical

Auditory

Smell

Nature

Taste

Tactile

Video Games

Vestibular

Humor

Proprioceptive

Interoceptive

The Eight Sensory Areas Explored

Using and processing the worksheet

Each of the eight sensory processing areas are presented in its own worksheet. Each worksheet begins with a writing/talking prompt to think about and communicate things that feel good and not good related to the specific sensory area. Each worksheet has a long box provided where the child or teen can write the good things and the not-good things.

Before the child completes the worksheet, it may be helpful if the practitioner/parent explains each sensory area in more detail. The practitioner/parent should utilize the descriptions of the sensory areas provided in the beginning of this workbook. If the child needs help writing, the practitioner/parent can write the child's thoughts in the boxes. The practitioner/parent may need to assist the child by providing him or her with some examples. If the practitioner/parent is aware of some good and not-good things the child experiences in a particular sensory area, the practitioner/parent can share those thoughts with the child to help the child think of more examples.

Once the child has completed the page, the practitioner/parent should process that page with the child, talking about where and when the child typically experiences the not-good things and where and when he or she typically experiences the good things. The practitioner/parent should note the not-good things, as these areas will become target areas to work on improving both the sensory processing area and specific environments/situations that are creating challenges for the child.

Seeing (Visual)

Write or talk about things that feel good and not so good when you see them.

Good

Not Good

Hearing (Auditory)

Write or talk about things that feel good and not so good when you hear them.

Good

Not Good

Smell (Olfactory)

Write or talk about things that feel good and not so good when you smell them.

Good

Not Good

Taste (Gustatory)

Write or talk about things that feel good and not so good when you taste them.

Good

Not Good

Touch (Tactile)

Write or talk about things that feel good and not so good when you touch or feel them.

Good

Not Good

Vestibular

Write or talk about things that feel good and not so good when you do activities that move your head or lift your feet off the ground (examples: somersaults, swinging, hanging upside down, and rollercoasters).

Good

Not Good

Proprioceptive

Write or talk about things that feel good and not so good when you do activities that move your arms and legs and use your muscles (examples: pushing, pulling, lifting, climbing, jumping, sitting, or squeezing).

Good	Not Good

Interoceptive

Write or talk about things that feel good and not so good when you have different feelings in your body (examples: heart pounding, hungry, stomach hurts, needing to go to the bathroom and being thirsty).

Good

Not Good

Sensory Processing Activity: Sensory Likes and Dislikes

Activity: Sensory Likes and Dislikes (by Robert Jason Grant, Ed.D, LPC, RPT-S, ACAS)

Sensory Target Area(s): Tactile, Taste, Olfactory, Visual, Auditory, Proprioceptive, Vestibular

Level: Child and Teen

Modality: Individual, Group

Materials Needed: Paper, Pencil

Introduction

Sensory Likes and Dislikes helps children and teens better identify what sensory challenges they experience and what sensory input can be comforting or pleasing to them. This intervention creates a visual reminder of positive coping skills the child can implement when he or she is experiencing a sensory challenge.

Instructions

1. On separate pieces of white paper, the child draws a picture of each of the following: a hand, a pair of lips, eyes, a nose, an ear, and the outline of a body.

2. On each one, the child writes things he or she likes and does not like that corresponds with each sense: touch (hand), taste (lips), sight (eyes), smell (nose), sound (ear), movement (body).

3. Once the child has finished writing, the practitioner/parent and child take each area, one at a time, and on the back side of the paper, write coping activities the child could do whenever he or she experiences something related to that sense the child does not like.

4. The practitioner/parent and child then role play, and the child practices experiencing the sensory discomfort and implementing some of the coping activities that were written down.

5. The practitioner/parent and child will discuss and role play all six drawings.

Rationale

This intervention provides a playful and visual way for children to work on decreasing anxiety and dysregulation that is caused by sensory processing challenges. The practitioner should have a basic understanding of what sensory challenges the child struggles with prior to completing this intervention. The practitioner/parent should be mindful of helping the child identify positive coping skills that he or she can implement when experiencing a sensory processing problem.

Sensory Likes and Dislikes Example:

(front: things that irritate or bother the senses)

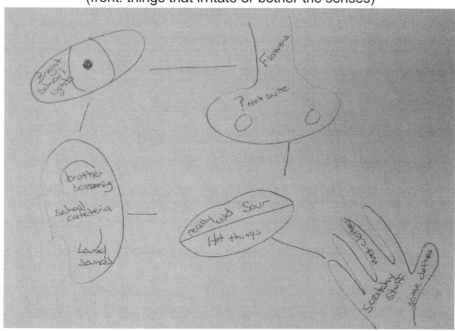

(back: coping skills for each of the senses)

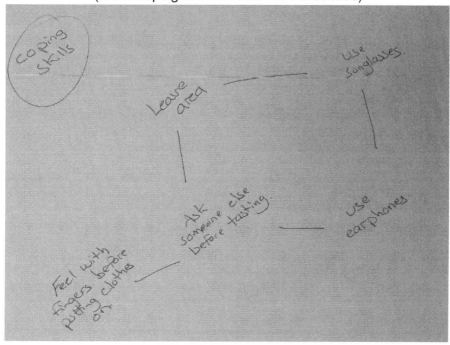

What Do You Think Are Your Biggest Sensory Processing Challenges?

Using and processing the worksheet

Once the child or teen has more formally learned about sensory processing and the eight sensory processing areas, he or she can complete this worksheet. The worksheet asks the child to list in rank order, from 1–8, the sensory areas that he or she believes are the biggest challenge areas. Whatever the child thinks is the most challenging sensory area should be written beside the number one and so forth. This worksheet helps the child begin to conceptualize his or her sensory struggle areas.

What do you think are your biggest sensory processing challenges?

Rank the sensory areas from 1–8 with one being what bothers you the most and eight the least.

(visual, auditory, smell, taste, tactile, vestibular, proprioceptive, and interoceptive)

1

2

3

4

5

6

7

8

Some People Have Strong Feelings When Their Sensory Areas Are Bothered

Using and processing the worksheet

Sensory processing challenges can produce many feelings. This worksheet provides several feelings and asks the child or teen to circle any of the feelings that he or she experiences when dealing with sensory challenges. The practitioner/parent should allow the child or teen to identify as many feelings as he or she can and then have the child or teen talk about each feeling that was circled.

If the child cannot think of any feelings, the practitioner/parent can try to help the child identify some feelings. It is important for children to understand the feelings they are experiencing with sensory struggles and be able to label those feelings accurately. Once children can do this, they can begin to manage the feelings and develop coping strategies to address the feelings.

Some people have strong feelings when their sensory areas are bothered.

Circle the feelings you have when you are experiencing sensory challenges.

Angry   WORRIED   Scared

Upset   Calm   Nervous

Overwhelmed   Happy   Sad

Excited   Anxious   Silly

Normal   Shy   AGGRESSIVE

Hurt   Pain   Relaxed

Some People Have Specific Behaviors When Their Sensory Areas Are Bothered

Using and processing the worksheet

Sensory processing challenges can produce many behaviors. Children and teens with sensory processing challenges often become mislabeled as behavior problem children when, in fact, they are dealing with sensory challenges that are creating the problematic behavior. This worksheet provides several typical behaviors a child may display when he or she is struggling with sensory processing. The child or teen is asked to circle any of the behaviors that he or she experiences when dealing with sensory challenges. The practitioner/parent should allow the child or teen to identify as many behaviors as he or she can and then have the child or teen talk about each behavior that he or she circled.

If the child cannot think of any behaviors, the practitioner/parent can try to help the child identify some behaviors. Typically, parents are aware of some of the behaviors that manifest when the child is struggling with sensory challenges. It is important for children to understand the behaviors they may display with sensory struggles and be able to understand why they are having those behaviors. When children and teens can understand how a problematic behavior results from their identified sensory challenges, this can be a very empowering insight for the child. Once children can do this, they can begin to manage the behaviors and develop coping strategies to help decrease the behaviors.

Some people have specific behaviors when their sensory areas are bothered.

Circle the behaviors you have when you are experiencing sensory challenges.

Yelling   Sitting Calmly   Jumping

Moving Your Body   Cursing

Talking a Lot   Saying Mean Things

Hitting   Running Away   Breaking Things

Asking for Help   Crying   Sleeping

Deep Breathing   Running Around

Acting Mean   Avoiding People   EATING

Sensory Processing Activity: Cotton Ball Guess, Soothe, and Fight

Activity: Cotton Ball Guess, Soothe, and Fight (Theraplay® Interventions by Evangeline Munns, Ph.D., C Psych, RPT-S)
Sensory Target Area(s): Tactile, Proprioceptive, Vestibular
Level: Child and Teen
Modality: Individual, Family, Group
Materials Needed: Cotton Balls

Introduction
Cotton ball games provide a fun, playful, and engaging process for the child to participate in and work on sensory issues. The whole family can participate in each of these games, and the games can be played repeatedly.

Instructions
Cotton Ball Guess
1. The practitioner/parent explains to the child that they are going to play a touching game using cotton balls.

2. The practitioner/parent and the child sit facing each other. The child closes his or her eyes while the practitioner or parent touches different body parts of the child with a cotton ball.

3. The practitioner/parent may touch the child's face, neck, head, ear, hands, fingers, etc. The child tries to guess where he has been touched.

4. This process can be repeated several times. The child may also have a turn at using a cotton ball to touch different body parts of the practitioner/parent while the practitioner/parent tries to guess where they have been touched.

Cotton Ball Soothe
1. The practitioner or parent explains to the child they will be playing a touching game using a cotton ball.

2. The practitioner/parent instructs the child to close his or her eyes, takes a cotton ball and smoothly and firmly touches the child's face all around the periphery of the face, the nose, eyelids, chin, etc.

3. While the practitioner/parent is doing this, the practitioner/parent states affirmations such as "nice rosy cheeks" as the practitioner/parent touches the child's cheeks or "strong chin" as the practitioner/parent touches the child's chin.

4. The practitioner/parent continues to facilitate the *Cotton Ball Soothe* until it seems like the child is no longer interested in participating in the activity.

Cotton Ball Fight

1. The practitioner/parent gives everyone participating several cotton balls.

2. The practitioner/parent explains that when he or she says "go" everyone will throw their cotton balls at other people calling out the name of the person they are throwing them at until all the cotton balls have been thrown.

3. This activity can be done with the participants standing, on their knees, or laying on their stomachs. The practitioner/parent can time the activity, having it last two minutes for example, and then begin a new round.

Rationale

These cotton ball interventions can be beneficial for children with tactile and vestibular sensory processing struggles. Some children may have an uncomfortableness with touch, and the touch process in this activity should be thoroughly explained to the child before beginning. This intervention should be implemented regularly to help improve sensory struggles. Many children with sensory issues may find this intervention relaxing and useful for a coping and regulating activity.

Several Theraplay® interventions can be used to help with sensory struggles. More information about Theraplay® can be found on the Theraplay® Institute website, www.theraplay.org, or in the book *Theraplay: Helping Parents and Children Build Relationships through Attachment-Based Play*, Third Edition by Phyllis Booth and Ann Jernberg.

Cotton Ball Games Example

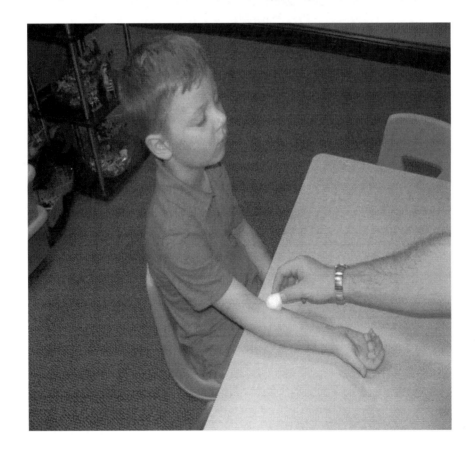

Who Helps People Improve Their Sensory Processing Challenges?

Using and processing the worksheet

On this worksheet, children and teens are asked to write who they believe helps children who have sensory processing challenges. If the child is communicating this verbally, then the practitioner/parent should write down what the child says. It is important to note who the child perceives as helpers and keep this list as support people in the child's life. If the child or teen cannot think of anyone, the practitioner/parent may provide examples of people who typically help children who have sensory processing struggles.

This is a good worksheet to introduce children and teens to people they may be working with, or will work with, who can provide services and support. It is important that children feel positive about the individuals they may be working with to help them with their sensory processing issues.

The worksheet also allows the child to recognize family members and friends as people who help or have helped the child. It also gives the practitioner working with the child the opportunity to communicate to the child how the practitioner can be a support for the child. Children and teens with sensory processing challenges need to understand and accept that there are people in their lives who will regularly provide guidance and support.

Who helps people improve their sensory processing challenges?

List some people you think can help you with sensory processing challenges.

_____

_____

_____

_____

_____

_____

_____

_____

_____

Sensory Processing Activity: Burrito Roll

Activity: Burrito Roll (by Cary Hamilton, MA., MFT, LMHC, CMHS, RPT-S)
Sensory Target Area(s): Proprioceptive
Level: Child and Teen
Modality: Individual, Family
Materials Needed: Weighted Blanket

Introduction

A weighted blanket is used to complete this activity. Weighted blankets are regular blankets that have been weighted to feel heavier. These blankets provide pressure and sensory input for individuals with sensory processing challenges. A weighted blanket can be used as a calming tool, as the pressure of the blanket provides proprioceptive input to the brain. This activity is helpful for sensory work and emotion regulation. Parents can implement this activity regularly at home to help their child stay regulated, and practitioners might find this activity helpful before and/or after a session where abreaction is present.

Instructions

1. The practitioner/parent explains to the child that they will be doing an activity to help regulate the child's body and they will be using a weighted blanket. (The practitioner/parent should show the child the weighted blanket and let him or her feel it before beginning the activity).

2. The practitioner/parent lays a weighted blanket down on the floor and asks the child to lay down on top of it.

3. The practitioner/parent then wraps the child up in the weighted blanket and instructs the child to lay still for several minutes; the practitioner/parent may lay down next to the child to cause less distraction and/or get on the child's physical level if it helps the child feel more comfortable.

4. The practitioner/parent then asks the child if he or she would like to be rolled across the floor in the weighted blanket; some children may be more open to this than others. If the child would like to be rolled across the floor, the practitioner/parent will do this a few times until the child is no longer interested.

Rationale

Weighted blankets work to help children regulate their bodies, and in turn calm their minds. The pressure of weighted blankets is beneficial to children who seek greater amounts of tactile input (hypo responsive). This activity allows for body regulation, particularly for children coming to treatment after school and those with ADHD symptoms. Having the parent assist allows it to become a connecting exercise and to ease transitions.

Burrito Roll Example

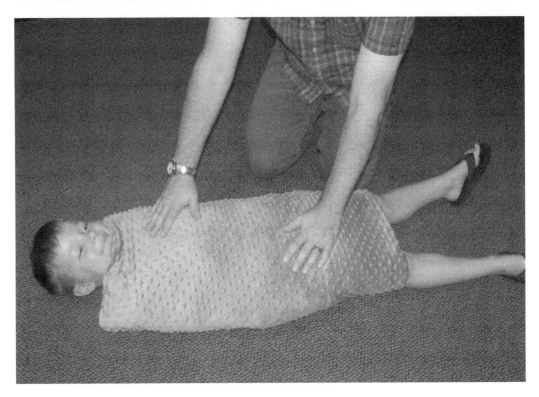

How Can You Get Better at Sensory Processing?

Using and processing the worksheet

This worksheet introduces children and teens to ways they can begin to address their sensory processing challenges to help improve their sensory processing. There are many activities and exercise that children and teens can participate in to help them improve sensory processing challenges, regulate their system, relax, and cope with their challenges. This worksheet lists some simple activities that a child or teen can do to help: using a stress ball, practicing deep breathing, doing body hugs and taps, doing toe touches, etc.

The practitioner/parent should explain to the child that there are interventions that can help the child with his or her sensory challenges. The practitioner/parent should practice each of the activities with the child and follow up after each activity asking the child how the activity felt. Did the child feel good completing the activity? Did the activity make the child feel more comfortable or relaxed? Did the child not like the activity? Did it make the child feel uncomfortable?

There are several interventions described throughout this workbook and several resources in the resources section for more activities and exercises.

How can you get better at sensory processing?

Let's practice 8 ways described below to help improve sensory processing.

1. **Stress ball** – Take a sensory ball, squish ball, or stress ball and squeeze and release it in your hand several times when you are feeling sensory struggles.

2. **Deep breathing** – Practice finger breathing by touching each finger to your thumbs and taking a deep breath (in through your nose and out through your mouth) for each finger.

3. **Body hug and tap** – Give yourself a hug and squeeze tight; keep the hug but release your tight squeeze and give yourself some alternating taps on your arms.

4. **Toe touches exercise** – While standing, bend over and touch your toes; do this five times.

5. **Wall Roll** – Find a wall with no pictures or other items on it. Stand against the wall, place your arms and hands in front of you on your chest. Roll yourself along the wall and back a few times.

6. **Sit and Relax** – Sit on the floor with your legs crossed and place your hands on your lap. Close your eyes and hum. Do this for a few minutes.

7. **Palm Press** – Stand or sit with your legs crossed. Put the palms of your hands together and press firmly. Stay in this position for a few minutes.

8. **Candy Crush Fun** – Take a hard piece of candy and suck on it and bite it while you think about something fun you like to do.

Sensory Processing Activity: Coffee Filter Mandala

Activity: Coffee Filter Mandala (From *Finding Meaning with Mandalas* by Tracy Turner-Bumberry, LPC, RPT-S, CAS).
Sensory Target Area(s): Olfactory, Visual, Tactile
Level: Child and Teen
Modality: Individual, Group
Materials Needed: Coffee Filter, Washable Markers, Small Spray Bottle of Essential Oil (preferably a scent the child likes), Cardboard, Table Cloth or Protective Covering, Black and White Construction Paper, and Paper Towels (for cleanup).

Introduction

This activity incorporates art and creation with sensory processing. Children and teens with olfactory (smell) struggle areas will enjoy this intervention. The practitioner/parent should explore with the child or teen what scents he or she likes before introducing this activity. The essential oil used should be a scent that is appealing to the child.

Instructions

1. The practitioner/parent will explain to the child they will be making a mandala using coffee filters.

2. The practitioner/parent will place the coffee filter on top of a white piece of paper, which is on top of a piece of card board or card stock for extra support.

3. The practitioner/parent hands the child some washable markers and instructs him or her to create any type of design on the coffee filter. The practitioner/parent may want to remind the child that this picture will change quite a bit, so it may be better to create colors and shapes rather than an actual picture.

4. When finished, the practitioner/parent will hand the child a spray bottle of a selected essential oil. The child is instructed to spray the coffee filter as little or as much as he or she desires. The practitioner/parent may want to suggest to the child to begin by spraying just a little and notice how the design begins to transform.

5. As the coffee filter changes into an abstract creation, the practitioner/parent watches with the child, noticing the aroma of the essential oil. If desired, the child can make additional mandalas.

6. The practitioner/parent may follow up with some processing questions such as: How did you notice your drawing changing while you were spraying it? In what ways can you change to help you feel better/more relaxed/regulated? How did you notice the spray scent as it was being sprayed on your drawing? How did it feel as you noticed the scent? Are there areas in your life you would like to spray away and start clean? Did you notice any feelings of calmness or relaxation while completing this activity? When and where in your life could you complete more coffee filter mandalas?

Rationale

Coffee Filter Mandala provides a non-threatening process to explore sensory processing challenges. This intervention can be repeated regularly. The child or teen can make several mandalas using multiple essential oil sprays. This activity may also be regulating and relaxing for the child and can become a part of his or her process for self-calming.

Coffee Filter Mandala Example

How do you Think you got Sensory Processing Challenges?

Using and processing the worksheet

This worksheet asks children and teens how they think they got sensory processing challenges. Many children will notice that they experience things that their peers do not and that there is something different about them. Likely, they will not understand the difference is sensory processing challenges, and they will not understand how or why they have sensory challenges and others do not.

The worksheet allows children to express what they think in terms of how they got sensory processing challenges. There is a circle provided where the child can write anything that he or she thinks. The practitioner/parent should note the child's response and be prepared to address any misconceptions or inaccurate information. The practitioner/parent will want to share accurate information with the child. Presently, there is no known cause for sensory processing challenges—some people just have these issues and have them in varying degrees. It is important that the child does not blame himself or herself or think he or she caused the sensory challenges. It is also important to help children avoid labeling themselves as less than or bad because they have sensory challenges.

How do you think you got sensory processing challenges?

Let's talk about or write in the circle below what we know.

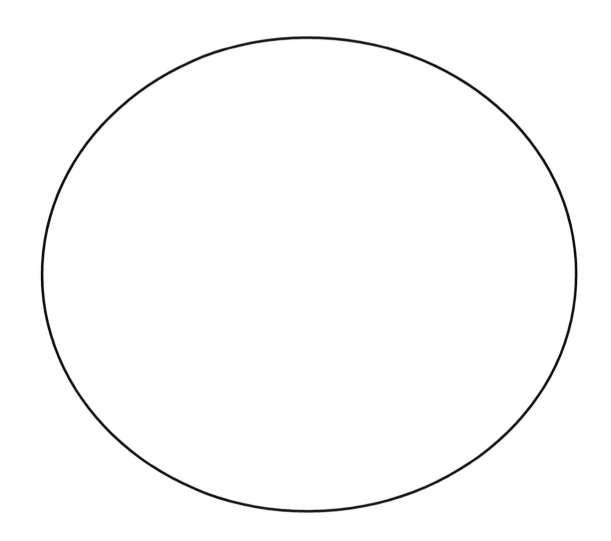

How Do You Feel about Having Sensory Processing Challenges?

Using and processing the worksheet

Feelings can be very challenging for children with sensory processing issues. Repetitive work on identifying and processing feelings of any type, especially those related to how the child or teen feels about having sensory processing challenges, is critical. This worksheet gives the child or teen the opportunity to identify and process his or her feelings. The worksheet is a guided illustration using a heart symbol to help the child identify what he or she feels about having sensory processing challenges. The child will color in the heart with his or her feelings about having sensory processing challenges. The practitioner/parent can use a feelings chart to help the child better identify his or her feelings. Several feelings charts can be found online.

Once the child has completed the coloring activity, the practitioner/parent can talk with the child about each feeling that the child identified. Specific focus should be placed on any negative feelings that the child identifies. Helping the child process through his or her negative feelings likely will require multiple conversations and/or interventions implemented via therapy.

How do you feel about having sensory processing challenges?

Color your feelings in the heart below. Each color represents a different feeling.

Sensory Processing Activity:
Bring on the Music

Activity: Bring on the Music (From *Positively Sensory* by Amy Vaughan, OTR/L, BCP)
Sensory Target Area(s): Auditory, Visual
Level: Child and Teen
Modality: Individual, Family
Materials Needed: Dry Erase Board, Dry Erase Markers, Music Player, Relaxing Music.

Introduction
Music is a great way to increase multi-sensory processing skill, ability to filter information, and ability to attend and shift attention. This activity aims to create a see it/hear it/do it loop for learning.

Instructions
1. The practitioner/parent explains to the child or teen they will be doing an activity that involves drawing on a dry erase board and listening to music.

2. The practitioner/parent draws a shape on a dry erase board and has the child look at it and name it. The practitioner/parent then covers the shape and the child must draw it from memory. This is done until the child can successfully remember and draw five shapes.

3. The practitioner/parent uses his or her finger to draw one of the shapes on the child's back. The child will picture it in his or her mind, name it, and then draw it on the dry erase board.

4. The practitioner/parent will add music (typically something relaxing such as Beethoven) and repeat the above sequence while the music is playing.

5. With the music continuing to play, the practitioner/parent will use his or her finger to draw two shapes in relationship to one another on the child's back. The child will picture it in his or her mind and then draw it on the dry erase board.

6. The practitioner/parent will switch from shapes to letters and keep repeating the activity until the activity time is over.

Rationale

Music can be a powerful tool. It can bypass our natural avenues for taking in information through regular pathways in the brain and often enters through our emotions. Using music for therapeutic change can be very powerful. Music can support and enhance the child's ability to engage in daily routines. Providing auditory cues in preparation for a transition can be as helpful as visual scheduling. This activity uses music to help children with sensory struggles and executive functioning issues. The activity can be played regularly to strengthen both sensory and executive functioning struggles. More information about Amy Vaughan's Positively Sensory program can be found at the website therapyspot.squarespace.com and through her book *Positively Sensory: A Guide to Help your Child Develop Positive Approaches to Learning and Cope with Sensory Processing Difficulty.*

Bring on the Music Example

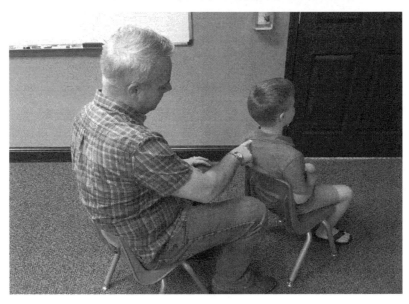

There Are Many Good Things about Our Sensory Areas

Using and processing the worksheet

There are many good things about our sensory areas and many positive things that children and teens experience through their sensory areas. This worksheet helps children think about their sensory processing in a positive manner. The worksheet presents a large blank book and asks the child or teen to draw a picture in the book having fun doing something while experiencing a sensory area.

It is important for children and teens to understand their specific sensory challenges, but they also need to realize there are positive things about their sensory system and to recognize some of those positive things. If the child or teen is struggling to think of anything to draw or write, the practitioner/parent can provide the child with some examples. Once the child has completed the drawing, the practitioner/parent has the child share what he or she drew.

There are many good things about our sensory areas.

Draw a picture of yourself in the book below having fun experiencing one of your sensory areas.

Let's Make a List of Things You Can Do to Get Better at Sensory Processing

Using and processing the worksheet

This is an exploratory worksheet; the child or teen is asked to list several ideas or things that could help him or her get better at sensory processing. The child or teen should be allowed to write anything that he or she wants and can think of—there are no restrictions. The child could write a person's name, playing video games, deep breathing, or playing with their pet. Once the child is finished thinking of ideas, the practitioner/parent can provide some additional thoughts.

This worksheet begins to form a list of strategies that can be implemented for helping the child with his or her sensory processing challenges.

Let's make a list of things you can do to get better at sensory processing.

This_____

And This_____

You Could_____

Try_____

Maybe_____

How About_____

Something Like_____

Probably_____

Possibly_____

Let's Do_____

What If_____

Sensory Processing Activity: Fun with Your Feet

Activity: Fun with Your Feet (by Kim Vander Dussen, Psy.D., RPT-S)
Sensory Target Area(s): Auditory and Tactile
Level: Child and Teen
Modality: Individual, Family, Group
Materials Needed: An assortment of surfaces of 10–12 different textures that can be walked on, some more pleasing than others to allow for a diversity of sensory experiences. For example, include a soft fleece blanket, a grass doormat, bubble wrap, a pillow cover filled with beans, a pillow cover filled with packing peanuts, a bamboo place mat, a course wool blanket, etc. These items should be arranged in a circle with sufficient distance so that the child can occupy only one surface at a time. Some music should also be playing in the background.

Introduction
Children with sensory processing issues often struggle with distal body parts like hands and feet. It is also common for the processing difficulties to be multi-sensory in nature. In order to help children with these processing challenges, engaging them in fun, pleasurable activities has been shown to decrease anxiety associated with these hypersensitivities.

Instructions
1. The practitioner/parent explains to the child or teen they will be doing an activity that involves a twist on the traditional game of musical chairs. Instead of moving from chair to chair, they will be walking across different surfaces barefoot or with socks only (dependent upon the intensity of sensitivity). Instructions should include something like "Some of these surfaces will feel really good and may even be fun, and some will feel a little bit uncomfortable."

2. The practitioner/parent may or may not participate in the play. This should be the child's choice. Allowing the child or teen to control some decision-making is an empowering process.

3. The practitioner/parent then explains that when the music is playing, everyone will move steadily across the different surfaces. Encourage participants to identify when they do or don't like a texture. When the music stops, everyone has to stand still on a surface, while one of the unused ones is removed.

4. The practitioner/parent should choose music with at least 80 beats per minute. Music with a distinctly positive message like "Happy" by Pharrell, "Can't Stop the Feeling" by Justin Timberlake, "Love Shack" by the B-52's, or "Walk This Way" by Run DMC are regulating and improve mood.

5. With the music continuing to play, the practitioner/parent will stop and start the song as if they are playing musical chairs with the surfaces becoming increasingly limited and individuals being eliminated from the game when spaces run out until a winner remains on the sole surface left.

Rationale

Sensory processing difficulties are reflections of fundamental brain functioning. Activities like *Fun with Your Feet* are designed to promote healthier brain functioning. The most adaptive interventions are relational (which makes people feel safe), rhythmic (which is consistent with brain patterns), repetitive (follows a predictable pattern), relevant (consistent with developmental level), rewarding (fun!), and respectful (mindful of culture, the family, and the child). Further information about Dr. Vander Dussen and her work can be found at www.drkimvanderdussen.com.

Fun with your Feet Example

What Does Sensory Over Responsive and Sensory Under Responsive Mean?

Using and processing the worksheet

This worksheet address two important concepts in sensory processing—being over and under responsive. The worksheet asks children and teens to identify what they think over and under responsive means. It is likely that children will not know what these terms mean. The practitioner/parent will want to explain the terms to the child and write down the basic descriptions on the worksheet. The practitioner/parent should reference the definitions provided in the beginning of this workbook.

Once the definitions have been presented, the practitioner/parent will want to spend some time talking with the child about his or her over or under responsiveness to sensory input. Helping the child understand the concepts and how his or her own system responds provides the child with a greater understanding of his or her sensory processing challenges.

What does sensory over responsive and sensory under responsive mean?

Talk about or write what you think

_____

_____

_____

Let's describe over and under responsive

_____

_____

_____

_____

_____

_____

Sensory Processing Activity: Digging Deeper

Title: Digging Deeper (by Mistie Barnes, Ed.D., LPC-S, RPT-S)
Sensory Target Area(s): Tactile
Level: Child
Modality: Individual, Family, Group
Materials Needed: Sand Tray (or other container), Sand (hypoallergenic is best)

Introduction

The goal of this intervention is to allow the opportunity to engage in and build tolerance to three forms of tactile stimulation (temperature, touch, and sand stimulation), while engaging in rapport and relationship building. Involve parents by encouraging them to be actively engaged in the "digging" process. This process allows parents to build rapport with their child on two levels: by interacting with their child in the digging process, and through the medium of touch as they work to uncover the child's fingers in the sand. The act of gently brushing the sand from the skin can be a bonding experience between child and adult.

Instructions

1. Begin by introducing the child to the sand tray and sand.

2. Encourage the child to become familiar and comfortable with the sand through touch, sound (listening as the sand runs through their fingers), and visually.

3. When comfortable, the child is encouraged to bury his or her hands as deep as they feel comfortable in the sand, and as much of the hands and fingers as the child feels comfortable burying (Note: Some may bury their fingers, their hands, and even part of their arms).

4. Encourage the child to experience the temperature of the sand, the coolness (or warmth if heated) of the sand against his or her fingers, against the top and bottom of the child's hands, and as it touches the wrists.

5. Suggest the child move his or her hand(s) and finger(s) in the sand, wiggle them around, and feel the sand moving on and around the hands and fingers, feeling the sand move around and experiencing the texture of individual pieces of sand.

6. After the child has had time to experience the temperature and feel of the sand, again encourage the child to re-bury his or her hands and fingers in the sand as

deep as they feel comfortable. The practitioner/parent will dig down to find the child's hands.

7. After the child has buried his or her hands and fingers and feels comfortable, the practitioner/parent will begin working in the sand. The practitioner/parent will begin gently moving the sand aside slowly, as they work to uncover the child's hand. As the practitioner/parent digs down in the sand, he or she will brush aside the sand as it covers the child's hand and fingers, allowing the child to experience the feeling of fresh air now touching the skin, and the gentle touch of the adult gently removing the sand from the child's hands and fingers.

8. The child will tell the practitioner/parent when his or her hands and fingers are completely found, and the child is ready to start over. For some children, they may choose to be free at the first sign of skin; for other children, they may choose to wait until the practitioner/parent has completely uncovered their entire hand and all fingers.

9. The practitioner/parent may choose to ask some processing questions such as the following: What does the sand feel like? Is it a good feeling or a not-good feeling? How deep do you want your fingers and hands to go? Does it feel better for your hands to be closer to the top, or closer to the bottom? What makes it feel better for your hands to be closer to the top/bottom? What does it feel like to move through the sand? When waiting for the practitioner/parent to unbury your hands and fingers, what did this feel like? Tell me about the feelings you felt in your fingers when the practitioner/parent was uncovering them? Tell me about the feelings you felt in your hands when the practitioner/parent was uncovering them? What were the feelings you felt in your body while the practitioner/parent was uncovering your hands and fingers?

Rationale

This activity is designed to build rapport between the practitioner/parent and child. It also builds relationship between the practitioner/parent and child. The activity allows the opportunity to engage in three types of tactile stimulation and increases tolerance to three types of tactile stimulation. This activity is designed to be used in individual (with the therapist as the one digging for the hands and fingers) and family (with the parent digging for the hands and fingers).

This intervention can be adapted to a group setting by presenting additional sand trays and allowing group members to work with one another. One individual will bury their hands and fingers, while the second individual works to dig their hands and fingers out of the sand.

This intervention can be adapted to a family group setting by providing additional sand trays and assigning each family group to their own sand tray. The family groups will then complete the intervention based on the general directions. Children may choose to cover not only their fingers and hands, but also part of their arms. Some children may be uncomfortable with the texture of the sand. Other options might be rice, beans, or a quantity of other small objects. Note: when working in high poverty areas, working with food items may not be appropriate, as individuals who are dealing with poverty issues may experience discomfort working and playing with food items.

Digging Deeper Example

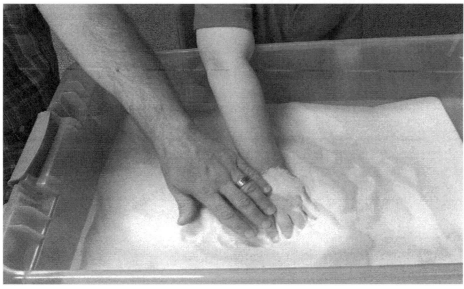

Some Places May Create More Sensory Challenges Than Other Places

Using and processing the worksheet

It is helpful for children and teens to understand that some environments may produce more sensory processing challenges than other environments. This worksheet explores a few common environments that children are often exposed to that may create sensory challenges. The environments listed are school, home, church, a party, and a restaurant. The child is asked to write beside each environment things in that environment that may cause sensory challenges. The practitioner/parent can add environments, especially ones in which the child is an active participant.

As the child identifies situations or things in an environment that create sensory challenges for him, the practitioner/parent should discuss with the child some strategies to help the child be more successful in the environment. This may warrant a larger discussion with staff or workers in the environment. Practitioners/parents are encouraged to try working with adults in the environment to strategize a plan for the child to be more successful with his or her sensory challenges.

Some places may create more sensory challenges than other places.

Let's name some possible sensory challenges for you at the places below.

School

Home

Church

A Party

A Restaurant

Sensory Processing Activity: Sensory Mandala

Activity: Sensory Mandala (by Robert Jason Grant, Ed.D, LPC, RPT-S, ACAS)
Sensory Target Area(s): Tactile, Olfactory, Visual
Level: Child and Teen
Modality: Individual, Group
Materials Needed: Card Stock, Scissors, Markers, Various Sensory Materials.

Introduction:

Mandala work provides children and teens the opportunity to engage in an expressive activity that can help regulate and relax their sensory system. A child can create a mandala on his or her own, as part of a group process, or in family work. The sensory element of a sensory mandala provides a unique blending of Jungian mandala creation with sensory processing technique.

Instructions:

1. The practitioner/parent communicates to the child that they will be creating a sensory mandala and gives the child a copy of a mandala template or creates their own. Using a card stock instead of paper may be preferred, as some sensory mandalas become too heavy for regular paper.

2. The practitioner/parent displays several sensory-related materials that the child can use in creating the mandala. The child is instructed to examine, touch, and smell all the items and choose the ones that feel the best to him or her. Sample sensory items include the following: Velcro, ribbon, sandpaper, buttons, beads, glitter, glitter glue, puffy stickers, potpourri, feathers, burlap, cotton balls, pom poms, pipe cleaners, denim, material (various textures), essential oils, spices, dried pasta, popsicle sticks.

3. The child is instructed that he or she can use markers or crayons and design and/or color anything in the mandala that he or she wants, and the child also needs to use the sensory items selected and place them in the mandala. The sensory items can be glued onto the mandala.

4. Before the child begins to create his or her sensory mandala, the practitioner/parent has the child take three deep breathes and begin to relax. The child can then construct the sensory mandala as he or she chooses.

5. The child creates the sensory mandala while the practitioner/parent observes.

6. Once the child has finished, the practitioner/parent asks the child to share about the mandala, specifically what sensory items the child chose and why he or she chose those items. The child can spend time looking at the mandala and touching the different tactile items the child chose for his or her mandala. If the child chose any scented items, he or she also can spend time smelling the different items.

7. The practitioner/parent discusses with the child that he or she can create mandalas anytime the child would like help feeling calm and relaxed, and the child can keep all the mandalas that he or she creates.

Rationale

Mandala work, from a Jungian perspective, can be a calming, reflective, and relaxing experience. Adding the sensory component enhances the sensory processing experience for the child. A sensory mandala offers an activity that is more expressive for children who respond to and enjoy expressive activities. Children can create a sensory mandala anytime on their own when they feel like they need a calming activity, or it can be part of a regulation/sensory processing break that has been established for the child.

Sensory Mandala Examples

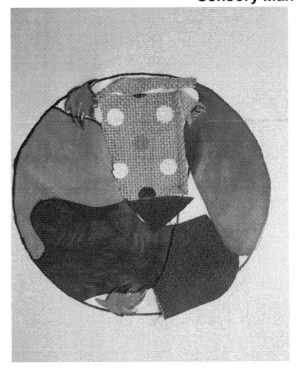 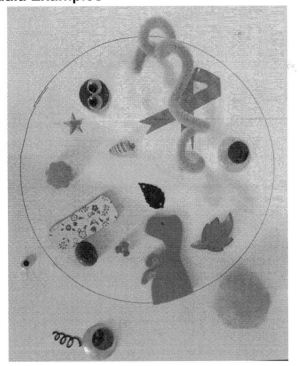

Write a Letter Describing what You Have Learned about Yourself and Sensory Processing

Using and processing the worksheet

As children and teens near completing this workbook, it is helpful to have them summarize what they have learned about themselves and sensory processing challenges. This worksheet asks the child or teen to write a letter describing what he or she has learned. The practitioner/parent should give the child plenty of time to write the letter. There are no restrictions, the child can write whatever he or she wants. Once the letter has been completed, the child can read the letter to the practitioner/parent. If the child cannot write, he or she can tell the practitioner/parent what the child has learned, and the practitioner/parent can write it down on the worksheet.

This is an appropriate time for any final questions or processing. Depending on what the child writes in his or her letter, there may be additional information to cover, or some subjects may need to be revisited.

Write a letter describing what you have learned about yourself and sensory processing.

Sensory Processing Activity: Sensory Rock Play

Activity: Sensory Rock Play (by Robert Jason Grant, Ed.D, LPC, RPT-S, ACAS)
Sensory Target Area(s): Tactile, Visual, Olfactory
Level: Child and Teen
Modality: Individual, Family, Group
Materials Needed: Various Rocks, Soap, Tub of Water, Paint Pins or Sharpies

Introduction

This activity incorporates art and creation with sensory processing. The activity is especially beneficial for children and teens who need tactile, visual, and olfactory sensory experiences. The practitioner/parent should prepare a tub of soapy water. The practitioner/parent can have several small-to-medium sized rocks prepared for the activity, or the practitioner/parent and the child can collect the rocks together. This activity can be a little messy. The practitioner/parent should prepare an appropriate space for water and paint.

Instructions

1. The practitioner/parent will explain to the child that they will be painting rocks.

2. The practitioner/parent will have a tub of soapy water, a few rocks (5–6), and paints or sharpies ready. The practitioner/parent explains they will begin by washing the rocks to remove any dirt. The child should wash the rocks and then place them on a dry towel (it may take a while for the rocks to dry enough to paint. If there is little time available for this activity, the practitioner/parent could provide a hair dryer to blow dry the rocks).

3. Once the rocks are dry, the child can clean and dry his or her hands. The rocks are then ready to paint.

4. The child is instructed that he or she can use the sharpies or paints to design the rocks however the child wants. The theme of the rocks is calmness and relaxation, so the painting of the rocks should reflect calmness or relaxation for the child.

5. Once the child has finished the rocks, he or she may take the rocks home and keep them to use as relaxation stones.

6. **Rationale**

   Sensory Rock Play provides the child or teen with a tactile experience of washing the rocks in soapy water. The practitioner/parent can experiment with different scents for the soap. The practitioner/parent also can provide scented markers or paints for a more olfactory experience. The coloring of the rocks provides a visual experience and a relaxation/calming activity. The practitioner/parent will want to make sure the child associates the whole activity and especially the painted rocks with relaxation. This is an activity that can be repeated multiple times with the child creating and collecting several relaxation rocks.

Sensory Rock Play Example

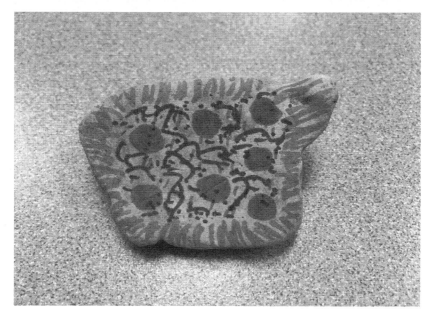

Whether You Have Sensory Challenges or Not, You Are Still Pretty Cool!

Using and processing the worksheet

This is the final worksheet in the workbook. It is time to celebrate the child being an awesome child. Regardless of any sensory challenges the child may have, we want him or her to feel good about himself or herself. This worksheet asks the child or teen to draw a picture of himself or herself being great! Once the child has completed the picture, the child should share what he or she has created with the practitioner/parent.

Whether you have sensory challenges or not, you are still pretty cool!

Draw a picture of yourself being great!

Resources

Sensory Profile

_____'s Sensory Profile

Top 3 sensory struggle areas

1

2

3

Things that feel calm & relaxing

1

2

3

My feelings when I struggle

1

2

3

My behaviors when I struggle

1

2

3

My sensory play diet activities

Sensory Play Diet

A sensory play diet is an in-office, in-home, or at-school protocol to help a child or teen improve sensory processing challenges, develop adaptive coping skills, reduce anxiety and stress, improve regulation, and provide playful techniques designed to increase calmness and relaxation.

The Assessment – Before implementing a sensory play diet, the child or teen should be thoroughly assessed to define the sensory struggles that are present. This may be done through a proper sensory evaluation conducted by an occupational Therapist. It will be important to understand what sensory areas are problematic and if the child or teen is under or over responsive in the struggle sensory areas.

The Pragmatics – If the sensory play diet is going to be implemented at home or in a school setting, it is important to establish where this will happen, when it will happen, how often it will happen, who will assist the child, if it is something the child will do by himself or herself, what activities will be selected, and what materials will be needed. The pragmatics should be decided by the professional working with the parent and others who will be involved. Likely, the pragmatics will look different for each child— tailored to the specific child's needs and abilities.

Where is the location (office, home, school, other)? Is there a designated space in the location where the sensory play diet will take place?

_____

When and how often (daily, every other day, once a week)? How long will the child engage in the sensory play diet activities: 10 minutes, 20 minutes, 30 minutes?

_____

_____

Will someone be working with the child, assisting the child? Will the child be engaging in all or some of the sensory play diet activities on his or her own, without assistance?

_____

_____

What sensory play activities will be done, and what materials are needed?

_____

_____

_____

_____

_____

_____

Sensory Play Diet Activities

The sensory play diet activities are a sample of activities. Each child should be assessed individually to determine what activities would best meet his or her needs.

Visual (sight)

- practice adjusting lighting
- look at lava lamps, bubble wall, or tower
- observe and identify colors in nature
- look at picture books
- experiment with different lighting
- play I Spy games
- make some glitter sensory bottles
- play peek a boo
- play with a liquid motion timer
- take pictures with a camera
- wear sunglasses
- wear a hat

Auditory (sound)

- play with musical instruments
- focus on and identify sounds around child
- listen to relaxation sounds apps
- listen to favorite music
- practice hearing tones (tone app or machine)
- use a white noise machine
- sing
- bang on pots and pans or other objects
- practice loudness of voice (whisper/yell)
- make silly sounds
- hum
- use headphones or ear buds

Olfactory (smell)

- smell flowers in nature or flower store
- take a smelling nature walk
- explore essential oils
- color with scented markers
- play a blindfold smelling game
- sniff spices and herbs
- make a craft out of scented potpourri
- have fun cooking together
- make a scented candle
- identify good smells and bad smells
- make a craft with scented stickers
- practice holding nose and breathing

Tactile (touch)

- play in a sand, bean, or rice tray
- give bear hugs
- use a weighted blanket or vest
- draw in shaving cream
- lotion hands or arms
- make pizza dough
- play in water
- play with finger paint
- massage
- play with putty or Play-Doh
- play with vibrating toys
- play with squishy balls and toys

Gustatory (taste)

- use a vibrating toothbrush
- blow a whistle or kazoo
- blow bubble in water with a straw
- play a blindfold tasting game
- explore food textures
- chew gum or suck on a lollipop
- eat hard candy
- play blowing games—cotton balls, bubbles
- explore food tastes—salty, sweet, bitter
- eat frozen, cool, and warm foods
- role play going to the dentist
- use chew devices—chewelry

Vestibular

- ride a bike
- bounce on a therapy ball
- swing
- play hopscotch
- dance
- do some jumping jacks
- run in different ways—fast, slow, silly
- do an animal walk around the room
- play catch
- do crab crawls
- do some backward moves—walk, hop
- climb some stairs

Proprioceptive

- do yoga moves
- play tug of war games
- push a vacuum or wheel barrel
- throw a weighted ball back and forth
- do wall or floor push ups
- mop, sweep, or rake leaves
- jump on a trampoline
- bang on a drum or ball
- do sit ups
- smash some clay
- hammer some nails in wood
- move furniture around the room

Interoception

Presently, there is no conclusive evidence pointing to one specific technique to support the development of healthy interoceptive processing in children. Researchers have suggested that body awareness, mindfulness, and behavioral techniques may help increase interoceptive processing. The following are some ideas. Interoceptive concerns should be evaluated by an occupational therapist.

- vestibular moves—swinging, rocking
- behavior modification schedules
- movement breaks
- meditation
- deep pressure activities
- yoga
- changing body positions frequently
- heavy work—pushing and pulling
- scanning and noticing body
- understanding emotions
- charts, timers, visual schedules
- labeling sensations and body experiences

Sensory Processing Screening Tool developed by Dr. Patricia Gilbaugh

Assessing for sensory challenges is typically done by a professional trained in occupational therapy or a medically-based physician. However, there are screenings methods practitioners/parents can utilize that indicate the probability the child has sensory processing challenges. Due to the lack of trained providers in rural areas, Dr. Gilbaugh developed screening guidelines that facilitate a better understanding of how much need is present for a child to seek the next level for diagnosing sensory processing disorder.

Based on the neuroscience triad structures, this screening was developed to assist as a guide and not as a diagnostic tool. Should a child screen probable as having sensory challenges, he or she needs to be referred to a primary care physician for orders to have an occupational therapist assess and develop the treatment plan.

Core Strength

1. Have the child stand facing you. Hold your hands out in front of you with index fingers in a pointing fashion facing inward toward the other hand. Have the child make a fist around your index fingers and instruct the child to squeeze as hard as he or she can. If the child puts forth a lot of effort, but results in minimal force with the squeeze, or if the child has to rock his or her body to exert the effort, the child would score moderate or severe loss of core strength on this item.

2. Have the child face you. Hold your hands up in front of you at the child's chest level, palms facing the child. Instruct the child to use his or her palms placed on top of your palms and push you as hard as the child can. If the child puts forth a lot of effort, but results in minimal force with the push, or if the child has to rock his or her body to exert the effort, the child would score moderate or severe loss of core strength on this item. If the child cannot push you hard enough to make you move at all, the child would receive a severe level of need for this item.

3. With the child still facing you, hold your hands up in front of you with your palms facing you sideways. Have the child grasp onto your hands in any comfortable position and instruct the child to pull you. If the child puts forth a lot of effort, but results in minimal force with his or her pull, or if the child has to rock his or her body to exert the effort, the child would score moderate or severe loss of core strength on this item. If the child cannot pull you hard enough to make you move at all, he or she would receive a severe level of need for this item.

4. You as the practitioner/parent reverse roles with the child, where you push the child and then pull the child. If you can move the child by barely pushing the child, score

moderate to severe with the loss of core strength on this item. If the child has a strong, stable resistance, the child would score no or mild loss of core strength on this item.

Balance and Coordination

1. Have the child stand in front of you, facing away from you. Using a ball (or balloon), have the child look up to grab the ball. Make sure the child has to look up and tip his or her head back. Have the child reach above his or her head with a small arch to the back. Once the child grabs the ball, have the child bend over to pass the ball back to you through his or her legs. Be cautious and prepared to catch the child should he or she lose balance and begin to fall over. Repeat in quick succession six times. A child who does not lose his or her balance after repeating the movement three times would score no or mild loss on balance and coordination. A child who loses his or her balance or stumbles forward would receive a score of moderate loss. A child who falls to the side or forward would be scored as a severe loss.

2. Have the child stand facing you. Have the child put his or her arms straight out from his or her sides. Ask the child to stand on one leg for as long as he or she can. When the child puts down the foot, have the child do the same with the other foot. If the child is successful with not losing balance, have the child close his or her eyes and repeat these steps. If the child is again successful without losing balance, have the child close his or her eyes and touch the child's nose with his or her index finger. If the child completes all of these actions without losing balance, the child would receive a score of no or mild loss of balance and coordination. If the child cannot complete any of these, he or she would receive a score of severe loss of balance and coordination on this item, and if the child can complete one but not two, the child would receive a score of moderate loss of balance and coordination.

3. Have the child stand in front of you with the child facing away from you. Hold up your hands to the child's mid-chest height. Have the child twist his or her body at the waist and use the opposite hand to high five your hand. Practice slowly with the child for about three high fives on each hand. Then repeat this *quickly* about five times with each hand. A child who can successfully accomplish this (hitting your hand on each side of him or her) without losing balance scores a no or mild loss on coordination. A child who does not lose balance but cannot hit your hand would score a mild or moderate loss on coordination. A child who cannot hit your hand, and who loses his or her balance would score a moderate to severe loss in coordination. A child who falls or stumbles, missing your hand, would score a severe loss in coordination.

In the case of screening for sensory processing challenges, the protocol is relatively subjective. Once a professional understands the expected developmental behavior for a neurotypical child, a child with sensory challenges will be markedly different than his or her neurotypical peers. Below is a table of comparison for most age groups.

Observational Setting	Neurotypical	Possible Sensor Affected
Sitting in a semi-formal manner.	Can focus while sitting still and upright. Can place hands in lap on a desk. Can follow teacher or parent with eyes or slight turn of head. Can keep legs or feet still. Can engage in a conversation without the use of body.	Has trouble focusing unless fidgeting. Hands and legs appear to "flail" or extend to the sides of the student. Turns body or twists in seat to engage in listening or conversation. Leans from side to side, rocks, or slouches when sitting to perform a task. Uses significant movements with body to engage in a conversation. Will frequently lean on caregivers to engage in conversation.
Movement around the room.	Can pick up an item from a shelf, examine it, and put it back on the shelf as it was. Can walk around the room without being clumsy or without tripping over items, floor, or own feet.	Feels a need to touch many things on a shelf before picking up one. Does not pay attention to putting the item back as it was found. Generally, walks about the room in a clumsy or tipped fashion, and frequently exhibits some type of tripping behavior.
Answering questions in the assessment interview.	Can answer age-appropriate questions with nods, verbal statements, or non-verbal gestures. Can communicate that the question was understood and will proceed with an answer. Exhibits minimal behavioral dysregulation.	Struggles to understand the question; will look at others for cues on how to respond. Will hide or express shyness or social anxiety due to lack of understanding. If provided with a kinetic object, will be able to focus better. Exhibits significant dysregulation according to how the questioning is perceived. The more anxiety provoking, the more dysregulation.
Sensory provocation.	Can be in the room without the need to touch, move, or put things into his or her mouth. Does not smell items before they are handled. Does not lick items before they are handled. Resists the urge to touch "fun" things, (per age appropriate behavior).	Will feel a need to touch, smell, move, lick, or put things in mouth. Cannot stay in a room in one spot and will want to touch anything that looks "fun", unique, or differently textured.

AWESOME Sensory Processing Books

Sensational Kids: Hope and Help for Children with Sensory Processing Disorder
– by Lucy Jane Miller and Doris A. Fuller

> This book highlights the latest research on SPD's relationship to autism, as well as new treatment options and coping strategies for parents, teachers, and others who care for kids with SPD. Other topics include the signs and symptoms of SPD; its four major subtypes; how the disorder is diagnosed and treated; and sensory strategies to help SPD kids develop, learn, and succeed in school and in life.

Raising a Sensory Smart Child: The Definitive Handbook for Helping Your Child with Sensory Processing Issues
– by Lindsey Biel and Nancy Peske

> Coauthored by a pediatric occupational therapist and a parent of a child with sensory issues, this book provides a plethora of information including how the senses actually work and integrate with each other, how and where to get the very best professional help, sensory diet activities, and practical solutions for daily challenges—from brushing teeth to getting dressed, from picky eating to family gatherings.

Can I Tell You about Sensory Processing Difficulties?: A Guide for Friends, Family and Professionals
– by Sue Allen

> This book is about a young boy named Harry who has sensory processing difficulties. Harry invites readers to learn about why he finds it hard to process sensory information. He also talks about difficulties he faces at school, explains how other people can have different sensory processing issues, and talks about what he and those around him can do to help.

Picky, Picky Pete: A Boy and his Sensory Challenges
– by Michele Griffin

> This children's picture book is perfect for any children with sensory processing disorder to help them better understand sensory issues. The character, Pete, finds his clothes and many other things uncomfortable. He explains this to his mother as he and mom navigate a difficult, but typical, morning in the life of a young boy with sensory issues.

Additional Awesome Books

The Out-of-Sync Child Has Fun: Activities for Kids with Sensory Processing Disorder by Carol Kranowitz

Sensory Yoga for Kids: Therapeutic Movement for Children of All Abilities by Britt Collins

AWESOME Sensory Processing Websites

sensorysmarts.com

> The website of pediatric occupational therapist Lindsey Biel. This website is full of helpful information and resources for parents and professionals. Interviews and articles are related to sensory processing. Practical solutions are provided for trouble areas such as teeth brushing, bedtime, bath time, and getting a haircut. There is also a handout listing several sensory diet activities for each of the sensory areas. Those wanting more information can purchase Lindsey Biel's books or attend one of her trainings.

sensory-processing-disorder.com

> The sensory processing disorder resource center is a plethora of information regarding sensory processing disorder. This website is a valuable link for parents and professionals. Several sensory processing disorder resources are provided, such as sensory diet activities, sensory products, occupational therapy information, and research related to sensory processing.

sensoryprocessingdisorderparentsupport.com

> Sensory processing disorder parent support is a community created by Jeanette Baker, a mother of two children with special needs. It is designed as a place to find support, get to know other parents who have children with SPD, ask questions, learn, share success, and spread awareness. The SPD community provides information for parents, caregivers, therapists, teachers, professionals, community providers, and all others who work with children and youth with special needs and sensory processing disorder.

asensorylife.com

> This website highlights the work of author Angie Voss, OTR. It is full of free sensory resources and tools. Many topics related to sensory processing are provided on this website, including sensory topics of interest, activities for improving sensory processing, and information on Yogapeutics, an aerial- and aerobics-based yoga for children and families.

Additional Awesome Websites

The Sensory Kids Store – sensorykidstore.com

Sensory Processing Challenges Effective Clinical Work with Kids & Teens – www.sensoryprocessingchallenges.com

AWESOME Sensory Processing Apps

Sand Draw

This app lets you draw or write on realistic sand. Several objects such as trees, weeds, rocks, seashells, and more can be added to the sand. The color of the sea, sky, and sand can be changed, and the texture of the sand can be changed. Children and teens can create their own design or create something working with another person.

Fluidity

A beautiful interactive real-time fluid dynamics simulation, control fluid flow and stunning colors are at the tips of your fingers. There are options of changing the colors, viscosity, and momentum. Children and teens can use their fingers to move the "fluid" around the screen.

Relax Melodies

This app provides dozens of sounds (river, ocean, instruments, wind, thunder, rain, white noise, etc.) that can play individually or simultaneously. You can save favorite combinations of music, set an alarm, and set a timer when listening to your selections. This is a great app for children and teens who need help with calming.

Heat Pad

This app simulates various heat-sensitive surfaces reacting to the heat of your fingertips. Relaxing and entertaining. Children and teens can play alone or meet other fingertips from all around the world and doodle on the same surface. There are several surface options, including heat, flame, fantasy, sky, metal, glow, etc.

Falling Stars

Children and teens can create an audio-visual show with just a few actions as they draw vines on the screen. There are falling stars, and when they hit the vines they play a note. Each vine plays a different note, and the falling stars hit them differently depending on how they're drawn. There are seven vine types included, and you can adjust the frequency of the falling stars by tapping them.

Additional Awesome Apps

Mandalynths	Zen Garden	Felt Board
Cove	Moving Child	Sand Art
Gloop	Fish Fingers	Kids Doodle
Anti Stress	Break It	Sensory Room
Breathe 2 Relax	Neutrino	Fluid

AWESOME Sensory Processing Toys

Sensory Trays

These trays can come in all sizes and types of content—a plastic tub filled with sand or an aluminum pan filled with shaving cream. Children and teens will respond to the sensory experience of moving and manipulating their hands and fingers through the sensory material. Some examples of tray content include sand, beans, water beads, rice, kinetic sand, moon sand, water, kay kob, dry pasta, and snow mobility.

Sensory Balls

These balls come in many sizes and many types of textures for a relaxing sensory experience. Most sensory balls are made of some type of rubber material and can be squeezed and manipulated in the child's hand. Try offering a variety of textures so the child or teen can choose what feels the best for him or her.

Liquid Motion Timers

A soothing visual display of liquid bubbling motion that the child or teen can hold in their hand, rotate and watch the fluid action. There are many brands, types, color, and variations of liquid motion timers. Most are small enough to be portable and held in the child's hand.

Mermaid Pillows

These pillows come in many shapes and sizes. They are made of reversible sequins. The colors change as hands and fingers move over or draw in the pillow's reversible sequins. Some pillows even reveal words or pictures as the sequin reverses. A relaxing and soothing product for children and teens.

Squigz

Apply pressure to two Squigz toys and they will stick together. A package comes with several shapes, sizes, and colors. They connect to each other and to any solid, non-porous surface. They assemble to become rockets, vehicles, jewelry, an octopus, etc. Great sensory experience of squishing together and pulling apart.

Additional Awesome Toys

Mini Trampoline	Wikki Stix	Weighted Ball
Tangle Relax Therapy	Whirly Wheel	Pipe Cleaners
Glitter Wands	Pin Print	Balance Board
Hoberman Sphere	Stretch Bands	Ball of Whacks

References and Resources

Auer, C. R., & Blumberg, S. L. (2006). *Parenting a child with sensory processing disorder*. Oakland, CA: New Harbinger Publications, Inc.

Ayres, A. J. (1991). *Sensory integration and the child*. Los Angeles, CA: Western Psychological Services.

Biel, L. (2014). *Sensory processing challenges: Effective clinical work with kids & teens*. New York, NY: W.W. Norton & Company.

Booth, P. B., & Jernberg, A. M. (2010). *Theraplay*. San Francisco, CA: Jossey-Bass.

Brady, L. J., Gonzalez, A. X., Zawadzki, M., & Presley, C. (2011). *Speak, move, play and learn with children on the autism spectrum*. Philadelphia, PA: Jessica Kingsley Publishers.

Burdick, D. (2014). *Mindfulness skills for kids & teens*. Eau Claire, WI: PESI Publishing & Media.

Cross, A. (2010). *Come and play: Sensory integration strategies for children with play challenges*. St. Paul, MN: Redleaf Press.

Delaney, T. (2008). *The sensory processing disorder answer book*. Naperville, IL: Sourcebooks, Inc.

Delaney, T. (2009). *101 Games and activities for children with autism, Asperger's, and sensory processing disorders*. New York, NY: McGraw Hill.

Dennison, P. E., and G. E. Dennison. (2010). *Brain gym teacher's edition*. Ventura, CA: Heart at Play, Inc.

Dorman, C., Lehsten, L. N., Woodin, M., Cohen, R. L., Schweitzer, J. A., & Tona, J. T. (2009, November 23). Using sensory tools for teens with behavioral and emotional problems. *OT Practice*. Retrieved from http://www.aota.org.

Garland, T. (2014). *Self-regulation interventions and strategies*. Eau Claire, WI: PESI
Publishing & Media.

Goodman-Scott, E., & Lambert, S. F. (2015, March). Professional counseling for children
with sensory processing disorder. The Professional Counselor, 5(2), 273–292.
doi:10.15241/egs.5.2.273.

Grant, R. J. (2017). *Autplay therapy for children and adolescents on the autism spectrum*.
(3rd ed.). New York, NY: Routledge.

Grant, R. J. (2017). *Play-based interventions for autism spectrum disorders*. New York,
NY: Routledge.

Grant, R. J. (2018). *Understanding autism spectrum disorder: A workbook for children
and teens*. Springfield, MO: AutPlay Publishing.

Green, E., Baggerly, J., & Myrick, A. (2018). *Play therapy with preteens*. Lanham, MD:
Rowman & Littlefield.

Kranowitz, C. S. (2005). *The out-of-sync child* (revised and updated ed.). New York, NY:
A Skylight press book.

Kurtz, L. A. (2014). *Simple low-cost games and activities for sensorimotor learning*.
Philadelphia, PA: Jessica Kingsley Publishers.

Kutsher, M. L., Attwood, T., and Wolff, R. R. (2014). Kids in the syndrome mix of ADHD,
LD, autism spectrum, Tourette's, anxiety, and more! (2nd ed.). London: Jessica
Kingsley Publishers.

Lara, J., & Bowers, K. (206). Autism movement therapy method. London: Jessica Kingsley
Publishers.

Lowenstein, L. (2016) *Creative CBT interventions for children with anxiety*. Toronto:
Champion Press.

Macintyre, C. (2016). *Strategies to support children with autism and other complex needs*.
New York, NY: Routledge.

Miller, L. J. (2014). *Sensational kids: Hope and help for children with sensory processing disorder (SPD).* New York, NY: Penguin Group.

Moor, J. (2008). Playing, laughing and learning with children on the autism spectrum: a practical resource of play ideas for parents and carers. Philadelphia, PA: Jessica Kingsley Publishers.

Myles, B. S., Cook, K. T., Miller, N. E., Rinner, L., & Robbins, L. A. (2000). *Asperger syndrome and sensory issues: practical solutions for making sense of the world.* Shawnee Mission, KS: Autism Asperger Publishing.

Pascuas, C. (2016). *The autism activities handbook.* Autismhandbooks.com. Schaefer, C. E. & Drewes, A. A. (2014). *The therapeutic powers of play: 20 core change agents.* (2nd ed.). Hoboken, NJ: John Wiley & Sons.

Star Institute for Sensory Processing Disorder. (2018). About sensory processing disorder. Retrieved from http://www.spdstar.org.

Star Institute for Sensory Processing Disorder. (2018). Your 8 senses. Retrieved from http://www.spdstar.org.

Vaughan, A. (2014). Positively sensory! A guide to help your child develop positive approaches to learning and cope with sensory processing difficulty. Springfield, MO: Scribble Media, LLC.

Walworth, D. (2012). Music Therapy interventions for social, communication, and emotional development for children and adolescents with ASD. In L. Gallo-Lopez, & L. C. Rubin (Eds), Play-based interventions for children and adolescents with autism spectrum disorders (pp. 317–332). New York, NY: Routledge.

Wilbarger, P. (1984). Planning an adequate sensory diet: application of sensor processing theory during the first year of life. Zero to Three. 10, 7-12.

About the Author

Dr. Grant is a Licensed Professional Counselor, National Certified Counselor, Registered Play Therapist Supervisor, and an Advanced Certified Autism Specialist. Dr. Grant completed his education from Missouri State University receiving a B.S. in Psychology and M.S. in Counseling. Dr. Grant further received his doctorate degree in Education from the University of Missouri. Dr. Grant operates a private practice mental health clinic in Southwest Missouri where he specializes in play therapy techniques with children, adolescents, adults, and families. Dr. Grant also specializes in working with Autism Spectrum Disorder, Neurodevelopmental Disorders, and Developmental Disabilities and is the creator of AutPlay® Therapy, an Autism treatment using Play Therapy, behavioral therapy, and relationship development approaches.

Dr. Grant has authored several articles, book chapters, and books about play therapy, Autism, and ADHD including *AutPlay therapy for children and adolescents on the autism spectrum: a behavioral play-based approach*. He is a professional board member for The Association for Play Therapy and conducts various presentations and workshops on topics such as play therapy and Autism. Dr. Grant has conducted trainings and workshops throughout the United States and internationally and has presented at various area and national conferences including the American Counseling Association, the American Mental Health Counselors

Association, the World Autism Congress, and the Association for Play Therapy.

Learn more about Dr. Grant and inquire about the trainings, products, and therapy he offers at www.robertjasongrant.com and www.autplaytherapy.com. You may also connect with Dr. Grant though Facebook, Twitter, LinkedIn, and Pinterest via Robert Jason Grant, Ed.D, and AutPlay Therapy.

Additional Products
by Robert Jason Grant, Ed.D

- AutPlay® Therapy for Children and Adolescents on the Autism Spectrum: A Behavioral Play-Based Approach

- Play-Based Interventions for Autism Spectrum Disorder and Other Developmental Disabilities

- Understanding Autism Spectrum Disorder: A Workbook for Children and Teens

- Let's Play: A Social Communication Book Game

www.robertjasongrant.com
www.autplaytherapy.com

The Virtual Sandtray App and AutPlay Package

The Virtual Sandtray App (VSA) is a new media interpretation of a physical sandtray. It is a new and exciting way to bring sandtray therapy to places not convenient for physical sandtray therapy, such as hospitals, disaster areas, in-home therapy, and travel. There are new opportunities to treat patients, such as those unable to physically access a standard tray, those who are unable to work with sand due to sensory processing reasons, and those who will not work with a traditional sandtray.

AutPlay® Therapy has partnered with the Virtual Sandtray App to create an AutPlay® Package. The AutPlay® Package includes models specifically chosen to represent the autism population. It also includes 20 directive sandtray techniques to implement with children and teens with ASD.

You can learn more about the Virtual Sandtray App at www.sandtrayplay.com. You can learn more about AutPlay® Therapy at www.autplaytherapy.com. You can purchase the Virtual Sandtray App on the Apple App Store. Once you have purchased the Virtual Sandtray App, you will have the option to add the AutPlay® Therapy Package.

Become Certified in AutPlay® Therapy

AutPlay® Therapy Certification is a curriculum-based competency credential. Certification in AutPlay® Therapy is a credential which shows that a person has achieved a proficiency and specialized training in AutPlay® Therapy. This certification is designed to establish a stringent and meaningful credential for professionals using AutPlay® Therapy. Its purpose is to demonstrate to consumers and referral sources that a person has achieved training, experience, and competence in AutPlay® Therapy, a comprehensive treatment approach for autism spectrum disorder, dysregulation issues, and other neurodevelopmental disorders.

There are Two Options for Obtaining Certification

Option 1: Complete an In Person (contact) AutPla®y Certification Training: You may complete an in-person (contact) AutPlay® Therapy training worth 16 hours of continuing education. In person certification is obtained by registering for and attending one of our contact trainings. Visit www.autplaytherapy.com for more information

Option 2: Complete the Correspondence (non-contact) AutPlay® Certification Training: You may complete the AutPlay® Therapy (non-contact) home based, correspondence training worth 16 hours of continuing education. Participants will receive and read the AutPlay® Therapy book, Nuts and Bolts book, and PowerPoint. Participants will complete a post exam that will be sent back to Robert Jason Grant, Ed.D ,AutPlay® Therapy Clinic. Participants can register for the correspondence training at any time at www.autplaytherapy.com.

Option 3: Complete a one-day Introduction to AutPlay Therapy training and finish the certification by completing an AutPlay Advanced day two training online. Visit www.autplaytherapy.com for more information.

Visit www.autplaytherapy.com for more training information. CAN'T COME TO US? WE WILL COME TO YOU! If you would like us to conduct an AutPlay® Therapy certification training in your area, please contact us at info@autplaytherapy.com.

Notes Sheet

_____

_____

_____

_____

_____

_____

_____

_____

_____

_____

_____

_____

_____

_____

_____

_____

_____

_____

_____

_____

_____

_____

_____

_____

_____

_____

_____

_____

_____

_____

Notes Sheet

_____

_____

_____

_____

_____

_____

_____

_____

_____

_____

_____

_____

_____

_____

_____

_____

_____

_____

_____

_____

_____

_____

_____

_____

_____

_____

_____

_____

_____

_____

Notes Sheet

_____
_____
_____
_____
_____
_____
_____
_____
_____
_____
_____
_____
_____
_____
_____
_____
_____
_____
_____
_____
_____
_____
_____
_____
_____
_____
_____
_____

Notes Sheet

_____
_____
_____
_____
_____
_____
_____
_____
_____
_____
_____
_____
_____
_____
_____
_____
_____
_____
_____
_____
_____
_____
_____
_____
_____
_____
_____
_____
_____

Made in the USA
Middletown, DE
25 March 2021